We have alread[y]
from the positio[n]

How great is the difference between a person who tries to overcome and one who withstands by knowing that he has already overcome. To withstand the devil means that we withstand him by the Victory of <u>Christ</u>.

Satan's strategy is to prevent us from having a thorough seperation from Egypt.

If you try to serve God in the world, you will surely end up being Satans slave.

Our heart + spirit are the first things that needs separation from the world.

Our Christian life @ a minimum should meet the standard of the worldly people we must refrain from things that Gentiles consider improper

Anything that is incompatable w/ the Lord <u>must</u> also be removed.

The Lord's relationship w/ the world should be our relationship w/ the world we can not take a different way.

Today there is no way for me to go to the world's side unless, I remove the cross

The world ~~My life~~ as soon as we open our eyes we will see nothing but the cross.

We only need to ask "what is my relationship w/ the matter and what was the Lord Jesus relation w/ it while He was on the earth.

Anything that is not on the same ground as the ~~or that stands~~ against the Lord is the world and we **must** depart from it.

Everything that quenches one's spiritual life in the Lord **IS** the world. The world is anyth that kills one's zeal for prayer to God. The wa is anything that takes away one's interest in G word." " anything that frustrates one fr testifying before men." " anything that hinder one from coming to the Lord, anything that results in confusion." " an atmosphere that chokes and dries a person up It is Anything that discourages from loving and yearning f the Lord

The
Uniqueness
of the
Lord's
Recovery
(3)

Witness Lee

The Holy Word for Morning Revival

Living Stream Ministry
Anaheim, CA • www.lsm.org

First Edition, October 2004.

ISBN 0-7363-2694-4

Published by

Living Stream Ministry
2431 W. La Palma Ave., Anaheim, CA 92801 U.S.A.
P. O. Box 2121, Anaheim, CA 92814 U.S.A.

Printed in the United States of America

04 05 06 07 08 09 10 / 10 9 8 7 6 5 4 3 2 1

Contents

Preface

1. This book is intended as an aid to believers in developing
   a daily time of morning revival with the Lord in His
   word. At the same time, it provides a limited review of
   the International Training for Elders and Responsible
   Ones held in Auckland, New Zealand, October 7-9, 2004.
   Through intimate contact with the Lord in His word, the
   believers can be constituted with life and truth and
   thereby equipped to prophesy in the meetings of the
   church unto the building up of the Body of Christ.

2. The entire content of this book is taken primarily from
   the published training outlines, the text and footnotes of
   the Recovery Version of the Bible, selections from the
   writings of Witness Lee and Watchman Nee, and *Hymns,*
   all of which are published by Living Stream Ministry.

3. The book is divided into weeks. One training message is
   covered per week. Each week presents first the message
   outline, followed by six daily portions, a hymn, and then
   some space for writing. The message outline has been divided into days, corresponding to the six daily portions.
   Each daily portion covers certain points and begins with
   a section entitled "Morning Nourishment." This section
   contains selected verses and a short reading that can
   provide rich spiritual nourishment through intimate fellowship with the Lord. The "Morning Nourishment" is
   followed by a section entitled "Today's Reading," a longer
   portion of ministry related to the day's main points.
   Each day's portion concludes with a short list of references for further reading and some space for the saints
   to make notes concerning their spiritual inspiration, enlightenment, and enjoyment to serve as a reminder of
   what they have received of the Lord that day.

4. The space provided at the end of each week is for compos-
   ing a short prophecy. This prophecy can be composed by
   considering all of our daily notes, the "harvest" of our in-
   spirations during the week, and preparing a main point

with some sub-points to be spoken in the church meetings for the organic building up of the Body of Christ.

5. Following the last week in this volume, we have provided a reading schedule for the New Testament Recovery Version with footnotes. This schedule is arranged so that one can read through the complete New Testament Recovery Version with footnotes in one year.

6. As a practical aid to the saints' feeding on the Word throughout the day, we have provided verse cards at the end of the volume, which correspond to each day's scripture reading. These may be removed and carried along as a source of spiritual enlightenment and nourishment in the saints' daily lives.

7. The training message outlines were compiled by Living Stream Ministry from the writings of Witness Lee and Watchman Nee. The outlines, footnotes, and references in the Recovery Version of the Bible are by Witness Lee. All of the other references cited in this publication are from the published ministry of Witness Lee and Watchman Nee.

International Training
for Elders and Responsible Ones
(Fall 2004)

General Subject:

The Uniqueness of the
Lord's Recovery
(3)

The Recovery of the Central Vision
of Paul's Completing Ministry

Scripture Reading: Acts 26:19; Col. 1:25; 2:2; 2 Cor. 4:7; Eph. 3:4; 5:32

Day 1   I. **"Do not take for granted that because you are now in the Lord's recovery, you are secure in the recovery and that it is not possible for you ever to be divisive. Whether or not we are secure in the recovery and protected from divisiveness depends on the vision we have seen"** (*Life-study of First Corinthians*, **p. 54**).

II. **The Lord's recovery today is the recovery of the central vision of Paul's completing ministry (Acts 26:13-19; Col. 1:25; Eph. 5:32):**

A. Paul was obedient not to a doctrine, a theory, a religious creed, or any theology but to a heavenly vision (Acts 26:19):

1. In this vision Paul saw the divine things concerning the dispensing of the Triune God into His chosen, redeemed, and transformed people.

2. Paul's preaching in Acts and his writing in his Epistles are a detailed description of the heavenly vision seen by him (v. 16; 22:15; Eph. 3:3-6).

Day 2   B. Paul's ministry was a completing ministry (Col. 1:25):

1. In the New Testament the apostles, especially the apostle Paul, completed the word of God, the divine revelation, regarding God as our content, Christ as the mystery of God, and the church as the mystery of Christ, thereby giving us a full revelation of God's economy (2 Cor. 4:7; Col. 2:2; Eph. 3:4).

2. Without Paul's completing ministry there is no way for Christ's heavenly ministry to be carried out, and without Christ's heavenly

ministry Paul's ministry would have no
ground (Heb. 7:26; 9:24; Acts 20:24; 2 Cor. 4:1):

a. These two ministries work together—the
one in the heavens and the other within us
(Heb. 8:2; Col. 1:25-27).

b. Paul's ministry reflected what Christ was
ministering in the heavens.

3. The goal of the Lord's recovery is the completion of the word of God; without the completion of the word of God, God's purpose cannot
be fulfilled, and Christ cannot obtain His
bride for His kingdom (Eph. 3:10-11; Rev.
19:7-9).

Day 3   C. In Paul's ministry, the completing ministry, there is
a central vision:

1. This is the vision that Christ, the expression
of God, has become the life-giving Spirit so
that He may impart Himself into us as our
life to make us living members of His Body to
express Him organically (1 Cor. 15:45b):

a. In His recovery the Lord is seeking to recover the all-inclusive Christ who imparts
Himself into the believers and makes them
His living Body (Rom. 8:10; 12:4-5; Eph.
3:17a; 4:16).

b. The Lord is recovering Christ as life and
everything to us and the church as His
Body, His fullness (Col. 3:4, 11, 16; 2:19).

Day 4   c. The central vision of Paul's completing
ministry is God in us as our contents,
Christ as the mystery of God, and the
church as the mystery of Christ (Rom.
9:23-24; 2 Cor. 4:7; Col. 2:2; Eph. 3:4).

Day 5   d. The center of the Lord's recovery is Christ
and the church: Christ as the embodiment
of God—the mystery of God—and the
church as the expression of Christ—the
mystery of Christ (Col. 2:9; Eph. 3:19b;
1 Tim. 3:15-16).

     e. The Lord wants a church composed of believers who are infused, filled, and saturated with Himself to be His Body for His expression; eventually, this living Body will become Christ's loving bride, who will prepare the way for His coming back (Eph. 1:22-23; Rev. 19:7-9).

     f. We should not care for insignificant things or be distracted by doctrines or practices; instead, we should care to become a living testimony by having the Triune God dispensed into us to make us members of His organic Body to express Him (Eph. 3:6, 19b, 21).

Day 6

2. We need to see a vision of the central matter in the Lord's recovery today (Prov. 29:18a):

     a. God wants us to realize that in Christ the Triune God—the Father, the Son, and the Spirit—has passed through a process involving incarnation, human living, crucifixion, resurrection, and ascension:

       (1) By incarnation Christ brought the infinite God into the finite man (John 1:14).

       (2) In His human living the Lord Jesus expressed divinity in humanity (14:9-11).

       (3) By crucifixion Jesus Christ terminated the old creation (Col. 1:15).

       (4) By resurrection He germinated us as the new creation (1 Pet. 1:3).

       (5) By ascension He was glorified, exalted, enthroned, appointed Lord, and commissioned with the divine government (Acts 2:33, 36).

       (6) Following this He came down upon the church as the all-inclusive life-giving Spirit (1:8; 2:4).

      b. As the life-giving Spirit, the Lord is waiting for people to receive Him by believing into Him (1 Cor. 15:45b; 2 Cor. 3:17; John 1:12-13; 3:15):

        (1) As soon as a person calls on the name of the Lord Jesus, Christ will immediately come into him, regenerate his spirit, indwell his spirit, and mingle Himself with his regenerated spirit to cause him to become truly one with Him (v. 6; 1 Cor. 6:17).

        (2) A new believer must come to know the two spirits—his regenerated spirit and the life-giving Spirit—that he may be transformed and built up with others to be the Body, the organism to express the Triune God for the fulfillment of His purpose (2 Cor. 3:18; Eph. 2:21-22; 4:16).

D. "What a mercy that we can see this vision! What a grace and what a wonder that we may be brought into the realization of this vision! We are burdened that all the saints in the Lord's recovery will see the same vision and then speak the same thing, having the same mind with the same opinion" (*Life-study of First Corinthians,* p. 185) (1 Cor. 1:10; Rom. 15:5-6; Phil. 2:2, 5; 3:15).

Morning Nourishment

Acts **For you will be a witness to Him unto all men of the**
22:15 **things which you have seen and heard.**
26:16 **...I have appeared to you for this** *purpose,* **to ap-**
point you as a minister and a witness both of the
things in which you have seen Me and of the things
in which I will appear to you.
19 **Therefore, King Agrippa, I was not disobedient to**
the heavenly vision.
Eph. **By which, in reading** *it,* **you can perceive my un-**
3:4-5 **derstanding in the mystery of Christ, which in**
other generations was not made known to the sons
of men, as it has now been revealed to His holy
apostles and prophets in spirit.

In Acts 26:19 and 20 Paul testified, "Therefore, King Agrippa, I was not disobedient to the heavenly vision, but declared both to those in Damascus first and in Jerusalem and throughout all the country of Judea and to the Gentiles that they should repent and turn to God, doing works worthy of repentance." Paul's use of the word "vision" in verse 19 indicates that Paul was obedient not to doctrine, theory, religious creed, or theology, but to the heavenly vision, in which he saw the divine things concerning the Triune God to be dispensed into His chosen, redeemed, and transformed people. All his preachings in Acts and writings in his fourteen Epistles from Romans through Hebrews are a detailed description of this heavenly vision he saw. (*Life-study of Acts,* pp. 603-604)

Today's Reading

In Acts 26:16,...notice that here the phrase "in which" is used twice. Here Paul is saying that the Lord had appointed him a minister and a witness of the things He revealed to Paul and of the things He would reveal to him. Although this is Paul's meaning, this is not the way he presented the matter. Rather, this verse speaks of the things in which Paul had seen the Lord and of the things in which the Lord would yet appear to him.

Acts 26:16 indicates that Paul did not receive the revelation of things without seeing Christ. Instead, he received the things in which he saw Christ. In other words, Christ did not reveal things to Paul without Himself as the content of those things. This is the reason that Paul would be a witness of the things in which he had seen the Lord. In all the visions Paul saw he saw Christ. Furthermore, he would be a witness of the things in which the Lord was yet to appear to him. Here the Lord seemed to be saying to Paul, "In all the visions and revelations you will receive, I shall appear to you." This indicates that if we only see visions and revelations and do not see the Lord, then what we see is vanity.

We do not agree with studying the Bible merely in a theological way. Those who study the Bible in this way may learn theology, but they do not see Christ. There is a great difference between studying the Bible to learn theology and studying the Bible in order to see Christ.

As Paul was on the way to Damascus, Christ revealed certain things to him, and in those things Paul saw Christ. The Lord indicated that He would reveal more things to Paul, and in those things the Lord Himself would appear to him. Therefore, what Paul saw was not merely the things themselves, but Christ as the One appearing in all these things.

In your experience you may claim to receive light from the Lord or to see a vision or revelation. However, you need to consider if Christ has appeared to you in that light, vision, or revelation. In the supposed light, vision, or revelation, have you seen Christ?

In any light we receive of the Lord we must see Christ. Christ must appear to us in whatever we see in the way of enlightenment, vision, or revelation. If we see a vision without seeing Christ, that vision means nothing. Likewise, if we study the Bible and gain knowledge of the Scriptures without seeing Christ, that knowledge is vanity. We all need to learn to see Christ in the things that are revealed to us. (*Life-study of Acts,* pp. 595-597)

Further Reading: Life-study of Acts, msgs. 68-69

Enlightenment and inspiration: That is the difference, a nouest has theory, knowledge, visions, revelations but when one see Christ there is life experience

Morning Nourishment

Col.   Of which I became a minister according to the
1:25-27   stewardship of God, which was given to me for you,
to complete the word of God, the mystery which has
been hidden from the ages and from the generations but now has been manifested to His saints; to
whom God willed to make known what are the
riches of the glory of this mystery among the Gentiles, which is Christ in you, the hope of glory.

In Colossians 1:25 Paul…speaks of completing the word of God.
The word of God is the divine revelation, which was not completed
until the New Testament was written. In the New Testament the
apostles, especially the apostle Paul, completed the word of God in
the mystery of God, which is Christ, and in the mystery of Christ,
which is the church, to give us a full revelation of God's economy.
According to 1:26, the word of God is the "mystery which has been
hidden from the ages and from the generations, but now has been
manifested to His saints." This hidden mystery is related to Christ
and the church, the Head and the Body. The unveiling of this mystery through the apostle Paul is a major part of the completion of
the word of God as the divine revelation.

Although the divine revelation was completed through the
apostles, especially through Paul, in a practical sense it also needs
to be completed through us today. This means that as we contact
people, we must progressively, continually, and gradually preach
the word in full. To preach the word in full, or to fully preach the
word, is to complete the word. Among so many Christians today
there is surely a great need for such a completing of the word.
(*Life-study of Colossians*, pp. 93-94)

Today's Reading

If we do not minister the riches of Christ to others, their knowledge of the divine revelation will be lacking. As far as the revelation
itself is concerned, there is no lack. Everything was completed centuries ago. However, in practice, there may still be a lack.

In the Lord's recovery we need more stewards who are able to complete the word of God. We all must bear the burden for this. We need to spend more time in the Lord's presence so that He may become our portion for our enjoyment and so that we may have the riches of Christ to minister to others. In this way we shall become those who complete the word of God. Then through our ministry other believers will be nourished, strengthened, confirmed, and built up.

In Colossians 1:29 Paul said that he labored, "struggling according to His operation which operates in me in power." Paul labored and struggled for the completion of the word of God. The Greek word indicates that he was wrestling, engaging in combat, for this completion....We also are wrestling for the completion of the revelation given to Paul. Apparently in the Lord's ministry we are working; actually we are fighting against religion with its tradition. We need to be clear, however, that our wrestling is not against blood and flesh, but against the evil powers in the heavenlies, against the gates of Hades that seek to destroy the church. As we struggle and fight, our burden, our stewardship, is to complete the word of God. What we are ministering today is the completion of the divine revelation given to Paul.

We need to point out again and again that this revelation concerns Christ as the embodiment of God and the church as the expression of Christ. Although there are a great many Christian activities in this country, there is hardly any completing of the word of God. Who is bearing the burden to declare that Christ the Savior is the life-giving Spirit imparting the divine life into us? Who is discharging the burden to tell the Lord's people that they should be the living Body to express Christ on the proper ground in each locality? We in the Lord's recovery must take up the responsibility for this. The goal of the Lord's recovery is the completion of the word of God. I hope that many brothers will rise up to fulfill this ministry. (*Life-study of Colossians,* pp. 95-96, 110-111)

Further Reading: Life-study of Colossians, msgs. 11, 13, 16; *The Completing Ministry of Paul,* ch. 1

Enlightenment and inspiration: I believe All who seek the Lord in a pure way has this burden to complete the word of God, b/c it is the goal of God not a personal fulfillment

Morning Nourishment

Eph. That by revelation the mystery was made known to
3:3-5 me,...you can perceive my understanding in the mystery of Christ, which in other generations was not
made known to the sons of men, as it has now been revealed to His holy apostles and prophets in spirit.
8-11 To me...was this grace given to announce to the Gentiles the unsearchable riches of Christ as the gospel
and to enlighten all *that they may see* what the economy of the mystery is,...in order that now to the rulers and the authorities in the heavenlies the
multifarious wisdom of God might be made known
through the church, according to the eternal purpose
which He made in Christ Jesus our Lord.

If we did not have the ministry of Paul, we would not know
God's eternal purpose or His economy. Although Peter was a
leading apostle, he does not tell us anything about the Body of
Christ. The highest word in Peter's writings concerns the partaking of the divine nature: "Through which He has granted to
us precious and exceedingly great promises that through these
you might become partakers of the divine nature" (2 Pet. 1:4).
In Paul's writings many terms are used to show that Christ is
all-inclusive and extensive, that He is the life-giving Spirit, that
He is everything in God's economy and everything to us. In his
Epistles Paul also reveals that the church is the Body of Christ,
the fullness of Christ, the dwelling place of Christ, the bride of
Christ, and even the new man. Furthermore, in his ministry
Paul tells us that we are in Christ, that Christ is in us, and
that we are joined to Christ as one spirit. In Paul's ministry,
the completing ministry, there is a central vision. This is the
vision that Christ, the ultimate expression of God, has become
the life-giving Spirit so that He may impart Himself into us as
our life to make us living members of His Body to express Him
organically. This is the central vision of Paul's completing
ministry. Paul is the only one to make this tremendous matter
clear to us. (*Life-study of 1 Corinthians*, pp. 181-182)

Today's Reading

The Lord's recovery today is the recovery of the central vision of Paul's completing ministry....In His recovery the Lord is seeking to recover the all-inclusive Christ as the life-giving Spirit who imparts Himself into the believers and makes them His living Body. In other words, the center of the Lord's recovery today is Christ and the church.

We realize that today what the Lord is seeking to recover is not head covering or any other doctrine or practice as a central thing. Rather, the Lord is recovering Christ as life and everything to us and the church as His Body, His fullness. We agree that immersion and head covering are aspects of the recovery, but neither of these things is the center. To repeat, the center of the Lord's recovery is Christ and the church: Christ as the embodiment of God and the church as the expression of Christ. This is what God is seeking today, and it is crucial that we all see it.

If we would fulfill the Lord's desire to have the proper church life on earth as His expression and as a preparation for His coming back, we must exercise our spirit to know the things of man, and we must also trust in the indwelling Spirit to know the things of God. Then we shall know that what God wants is not speaking in tongues, healing, or miraculous gifts. The Lord has recovered these matters, but they are not the center or the goal of His recovery. What the Lord wants is not tongue-speaking, healing, or the lengthening of legs; He wants a church composed of believers who are filled, saturated, and infused with Himself to be His Body for His expression. For this, we need the real experience of the indwelling Spirit, not merely the outward gifts of the Spirit. (*Life-study of 1 Corinthians,* pp. 182-184)

Further Reading: Life-study of 1 Corinthians, msg. 20

Enlightenment and inspiration: _____

_____

_____

_____

Morning Nourishment

**Rom. In order that He might make known the riches of
9:23 His glory upon vessels of mercy, which He had before prepared unto glory.**

**2 Cor. But we have this treasure in earthen vessels that
4:7 the excellency of the power may be of God and not
out of us.**

**Eph. ...That you may be filled unto all the fullness of God.
3:19**

[Remember] these three crucial points in Paul's Epistles: God
as our contents, Christ as God's mystery, and the church as
Christ's mystery. Without these three points, Paul's writings are
an empty shell. These are what the Lord is going to recover. Without them, nothing is meaningful. Our God today is in us to be our
contents. The mystery of God is Christ as the embodiment and
manifestation of God, making God so real and so enjoyable to us.
The mystery of Christ is that the Triune God through death and
in resurrection is mingling Himself with us, making us the living
members of His organic Body. This vision must direct us. It will
keep us in the central lane, walking according to the mingled
spirit and being in the Body life. This is what the Lord is after.

We need some faithful ones to rise up and say, "Lord, here I am.
Show me the central vision as you did with the apostle Paul." I
hope you younger ones, especially those who are in their twenties,
will do this. Then after ten years you will be valuable to the Lord's
recovery. (*The Completing Ministry of Paul,* pp. 107, 96)

Today's Reading

When Paul refers to God, he of course says that God is the Cre-
ator (Rom. 1:25), but this is not his central point....Let us consider
Romans 9:23-24: "In order that He might make known the riches
of His glory upon vessels of mercy, which He had before prepared
unto glory, even us, whom He has also called...?" We are here
called vessels. God has chosen us to be His vessels, vessels of
mercy unto glory. This implies and indicates that God wants to be
contained; He wants a container for Himself.

Seldom does the thought cross our mind that we are a vessel to contain God. All too often, however, we entertain the thought that we must behave rightly, courteously, humbly, and inoffensively. Day after day we are sorry not to be more obedient to our parents, more pleasant to our classmates, and kinder to our sister or brother. We may think along even more spiritual lines, about getting up early for morning watch or spending more time to read the Bible. Such thoughts are commonplace to us. But how about the thought that we are vessels to contain God? Does this thought occur to us? We may obey our parents and love our sister but not have God contained in us. If so, we are like an empty box, trying to please others but apart from God....Whenever we think in terms of loving others or being kind, without realizing that we were ordained to contain God, we...are missing the mark. We must learn to turn away from all such considerations of behavior and care only to be filled with God.

Ephesians 3:19b says, "That you may be filled unto all the fullness of God." To be filled unto all God's fullness means to be filled unto all that God is. This fullness dwells in Christ (Col. 1:19; 2:9). Through His indwelling, Christ imparts the fullness of God into our being. This makes us God's expression. The fullness of God implies that the riches of what He is become His expression. When the riches are in Him, they are His riches; when they are expressed, they become His fullness. All that God is should be our contents. We should be so filled with Him that we become His fullness, His expression.

To become God's fullness is in a category entirely apart from being kind and humble. These past three years I have several times repented for being outwardly blameless while I was not filled with the Lord. "Lord," I have prayed, "forgive me. I failed You today....I helped the church, but I was not filled with You....Forgive me for all the good things I did apart from You as my contents." We all need to become aware of this distinction between being good and being filled with the Lord. (*The Completing Ministry of Paul,* pp. 75-78)

Further Reading: The Completing Ministry of Paul, chs. 10-12

Enlightenment and inspiration: _____

_____

_____

_____

Morning Nourishment

Col. That their hearts may be comforted, they being knit
2:2 together in love and unto all the riches of the full assurance of understanding, unto the full knowledge
of the mystery of God, Christ.

Eph. By which, in reading *it*, you can perceive my under-
3:4 standing in the mystery of Christ.
6 That in Christ Jesus the Gentiles are fellow heirs
and fellow members of the Body and fellow partakers of the promise through the gospel.
5:32 This mystery is great, but I speak with regard to
Christ and the church.

The mystery of the universe is God. The mystery of God, the New Testament reveals, is Christ (Col. 2:2). The mystery of Christ is the church (Eph. 3:4)....God is a mystery, and Christ, as the embodiment of God to express Him, is the mystery of God. Christ is also a mystery, and the church, as the Body of Christ to express Him, is the mystery of Christ.

According to Ephesians 3:4, the church has a particular title—the mystery of Christ. When we consider Ephesians 3:4 in context, we see that the mystery of Christ is the church. Thus, Christ is the mystery of God, and the church is the mystery of Christ. God is a mystery, Christ is the mystery of God, and the church is the mystery of Christ. Hence, the church is actually a mystery within a mystery, for the church is a mystery in the third stage. The first stage is God Himself as the mystery of the universe; the second stage is Christ as the mystery of God; and the third stage is the church as the mystery of Christ. (*The Conclusion of the New Testament*, pp. 2053-2054)

Today's Reading

In God's economy revealed in the New Testament there are mainly two mysteries. The first mystery...is Christ as the mystery of God. In Colossians 2:2 Paul speaks of the "full knowledge of the mystery of God, Christ." Christ is God's mystery. In Himself God is a mystery. He is real, living, and almighty; however, He is invisible. Because no one has ever seen God, He is a mystery. This mysterious God is embodied in Christ. Hence, Christ is the mystery of God. Christ is not only God, but He is God embodied, God defined, God explained, and God expressed. Therefore, Christ is God made visible. The Lord Jesus said, "He who has seen Me has seen the Father" (John 14:9). The first mystery in God's economy is Christ, God expressed, as the mystery of God.

The second mystery...is the mystery of Christ. Christ also is a mystery. In Ephesians 3:4 Paul uses the expression "the mystery of Christ." Furthermore, Colossians 1:27 says, "To whom God willed to make known what are the riches of the glory of this mystery among the Gentiles, which is Christ in you, the hope of glory." As believers, we have Christ dwelling in us. But this Christ whom we have is a mystery. Although Christ lives in us, worldly people do not realize that He is in us. To them, this is a mystery. But although Christ is mysterious, the church is the manifestation of Christ. As the Body of Christ, the church is the expression of Christ. When we see the church, we see Christ. When we come into the church, we come into Christ. When we contact the church, we contact Christ. The church is truly the mystery of Christ.

As a mystery, the church is in the Triune God, in the Father, in the Son, and in the Spirit. With the believers there is an amount of mystery, but not as much as with the church. The divine mystery is much more with the church corporately than with the believers individually. The church is a corporate unit produced out of Christ, who is the mystery of God. This all-inclusive Christ is the mystery of the mysterious God, and such a Christ as the mystery of God produces a unit which is the church. By this we can realize that the church is the continuation of the mystery which is Christ. Mystery surely produces mystery. Christ, who is the mystery of God, brings forth the church, the mystery of Christ. (*The Conclusion of the New Testament,* pp. 2054-2055)

Further Reading: The Conclusion of the New Testament, msgs. 189-204; *The World Situation and God's Move,* chs. 5-6

Enlightenment and inspiration: _____

_____

_____

_____

Morning Nourishment

Prov. Where there is no vision, the people cast off re-
29:18 straint...
Eph. Out from whom all the Body, being joined together
4:16 and being knit together *through* every joint of the
rich supply and through the operation in the measure of each one part, causes the growth of the
Body unto the building up of itself in love.

God wants us to realize that the Triune God—the Father, the
Son, and the Spirit—has passed through a process involving incarnation, human living, crucifixion, resurrection, and ascension. By crucifixion, Jesus Christ terminated the old creation. By
resurrection, He germinated us in the new creation. By ascension, He was glorified, exalted, enthroned, appointed Lord, and
commissioned with the divine government. Following this, He
came down upon the church as the all-inclusive life-giving
Spirit. Today, as this Spirit, He is waiting for people to receive
Him by believing in Him. As soon as a person calls on the name
of the Lord Jesus, Christ will immediately come into him, regen-
erate his spirit, indwell his spirit, and mingle Himself with his
regenerated spirit to cause him to become truly one with Him.
Then this new believer must come to know his spirit and also
the life-giving Spirit, the ultimate expression of the Triune
God, that he may be transformed and built up with others to
be the Body, the organism to express the Triune God for the fulfillment of God's purpose. This is God's goal, the center of His
recovery today. (*Life-study of 1 Corinthians*, p. 184)

Today's Reading

We in the Lord's recovery, therefore, should not care for
insignificant things or be distracted by doctrines or practices.
We should care only to become a living testimony by having
the Triune God dispensed into us to make us members of His
organic Body to express Him.

We do not expect that the majority of Christians will see this
vision or take this way. But we do believe that it is of the Lord that

a minority of His chosen people, who love Him and seek Him, will be brought into this central vision that they may grow in life and be transformed by the Spirit to become parts of the living Body of Christ. Eventually, this living Body will become Christ's loving bride, who will prepare the way for His coming back.

In the first two chapters of 1 Corinthians Paul paves the way for us to see the central vision of His completing ministry. In these chapters Paul helps us to see the position, condition, situation, and destiny of the believers. If we are clear about these matters, we shall drop all natural things—our philosophy, wisdom, and culture. We shall not care for our attainments, but only for our position in Christ and our condition, situation, and destiny in Him. We shall also care for the genuine experience of the Triune God and for the enjoyment of Christ, the Son of God. By the Spirit in our spirit we shall know God and all the things of God, which are actually Christ Himself. We shall see that God's power, and even His weakness, is Christ....Now Christ today is our power and wisdom from God. Furthermore, He is our daily righteousness, sanctification, and redemption. We may even know Him as the depths of God. In this way we know all the things of God.

By our spirit we know the things of man, and by God's Spirit we know the things of God. As a result, we can live in Christ, with Christ, by Christ, and for Christ. Then He will have the proper church life as His organic Body to express Him.

What a mercy that we can see this vision! What a grace and what a wonder that we may be brought into the realization of this vision! We are burdened that all the saints in the Lord's recovery will see the same vision and then speak the same thing, having the same mind with the same opinion. (*Life-study of 1 Corinthians,* pp. 184-185)

Further Reading: Life-study of 1 Corinthians, msg. 20; *The Practical Way to Live a Life according to the High Peak of the Divine Revelation in the Holy Scriptures,* chs. 4, 6*

Enlightenment and inspiration: _____

_____
_____
_____

Hymns, #818

1   Christ is the mystery of God;
     God is invisible, unshown,
     His image man hath never seen,
     But Christ the Son hath made Him known.

2   Christ is the very Word of God,
     He is God's explanation true;
     God's full embodiment is He
     And God's own image brings to view.

3   Image of God invisible,
     Effulgence of God's glory fair;
     God's fulness ever dwells in Him,
     God's testimony He doth bear.

4   The Church the myst'ry is of Christ,
     For He is now to man unshown;
     No man on earth may see Him now,
     But thru the Church He is made known.

5   The Church is Christ's expression full,
     In her Christ dwelleth bodily;
     She is His duplication true,
     And man in her Himself may see.

6   The Church the image has of Christ,
     She is His increase and His spread;
     Christ's very self is found in her,
     The Body, she, to Christ the Head.

7   Thus, in the Son the Father is,
     And now the Spirit is the Son;
     The Spirit of the triune God
     Is in the Church and with her one.

Composition for prophecy with main point and sub-points: _____

_____

_____

_____

_____

_____

_____

_____

_____

_____

_____

_____

_____

_____

_____

_____

_____

_____

_____

_____

_____

_____

_____

_____

_____

_____

_____

_____

_____

_____

_____

_____

_____

_____

_____

_____

_____

The Unique Oneness of the Body of Christ—
the Oneness in the Triune God

Scripture Reading: Exo. 26:15, 24-29; John 17:11, 21-23; Eph. 4:2-3

Day 1   I. The oneness of the Body of Christ is the oneness in the Triune God revealed in the Lord's prayer in John 17; the oneness of the Body of Christ is the enlarged oneness of the Divine Trinity (vv. 11, 21-23).

II. The oneness for which the Lord prayed in John 17 is the oneness typified by the tabernacle in Exodus 26; because the forty-eight boards of the tabernacle typify the believers built together to be the dwelling place of God, the tabernacle is a clear picture of the oneness in the Triune God:

A. The first aspect of the oneness in the Triune God is seen with the three gold rings (the receptacles for the uniting bars), which signify the initial Spirit, the regenerating and sealing Spirit, the all-inclusive Spirit of the Triune God in resurrection for the uniting of the believers (Exo. 26:15, 24, 29; John 3:6; Eph. 1:13; 4:3, 30; cf. Gen. 24:22; Luke 15:22).

Day 2   B. The second aspect of the oneness in the Triune God is seen in the overlaying of the boards (signifying the believers with the human nature) with gold (signifying God with the divine nature) (Exo. 26:29):

1. The oneness of the boards of the tabernacle was not in the acacia wood but in the gold that overlaid the wood; this portrays that the oneness in the church is not in our humanity but in the Triune God with His divine nature (John 17:21).

2. The oneness of the boards was not only in the gold, signifying God, but also in the

shining of the gold, the expression of the gold, signifying the glory of God; our oneness today is in the Triune God and in His glory, His shining, His expression (vv. 22-24).

3. The initial Spirit, who is the Triune God typified by the gold, is the oneness of the Spirit (Eph. 4:3); the overlaying of the gold is actually the spreading of the oneness:

   a. The more we are overlaid with gold, the more oneness we have; the more we have of God, the stronger our oneness is (cf. Col. 2:19).

   b. Instead of being overlaid with gold, we may be merely gilded with gold, like Babylon the Great in Revelation 17; the amount of gold we have may not be enough to keep us in the genuine oneness (v. 4).

   c. Only when the boards were adequately overlaid with gold were they perfected into one; this indicates that to be perfected into one is to gain more of God (John 17:23).

Day 3

4. "Not having an adequate amount of God can create a serious problem with the oneness. The Lord's recovery is not a movement. We do not desire to gain a large number of people. In the recovery we are concerned for the genuine weight of gold. The important question is this: How much of God do you have? The Lord's recovery consists of God overlaying His recovered people with Himself" (*Truth Messages*, pp. 88-89).

5. Oneness is a matter of sinking deeply into the Triune God until we are fully overlaid with gold; our problem is that we are short

of God and our need is to gain more of Him
(Col. 2:19b; Phil. 3:8b):

a. Everything depends upon how much
gold we have; we all can become dissenting if we are short of gold.

b. Today the Lord needs this genuine oneness; if we do not have this oneness, we
cannot go on in the recovery.

c. The only way to be kept in this solid, real
oneness is to have an adequate amount
of the experienced God (v. 10).

Day 4   6. The golden nature of God will never overlay
our fallen nature but will overlay only our
regenerated and transformed nature, signified by acacia wood:

a. The overlaying of gold occurs simulta-
neously with this transformation; wherever transformation is, there the overlaying of the gold is also.

b. Transformation depends upon our loving the Lord, our contacting Him, our
listening to His word, our praying to
Him, and our walking according to the
spirit; as long as we have these five
things, we are living Christ (Rom. 8:4;
Phil. 1:19-21a).

c. Only when we all have been transformed
and overlaid with gold will it no longer
be possible for there to be dissension
among us; the only safeguard is to be
overlaid with gold (2 Cor. 3:18; Rom.
12:2).

Day 5   C. The third aspect of the oneness in the Triune
&   God is seen with the uniting bars, which held
Day 6   the forty-eight boards together and brought
them into oneness; these uniting bars signify
the initial Spirit becoming the uniting Spirit to
join all the members of Christ into one Body
(Exo. 26:26-29; Eph. 4:3):

1. The uniting bars were made of acacia wood for connecting strength and overlaid with gold for uniting; that the bars were made of acacia wood indicates that the oneness of the Spirit involves not only Christ's divinity but also His humanity (cf. v. 2, note 1, Recovery Version).

2. In actuality, the uniting bars signify not the Holy Spirit alone, but the Holy Spirit mingled with our human spirit (Rom. 8:16)—the mingled spirit, which includes both divinity and humanity.

3. The uniting of the boards of the tabernacle involved the passing of the bars through the rings on each board to join the boards together; this signifies that the believers in Christ are united when their spirit cooperates with the Spirit, thus allowing the uniting Spirit to pass through them to join them to other believers.

4. In order for the uniting Spirit to pass through us and thus join us with others, we need to receive the cross, for the uniting Spirit always crosses the standing boards (Matt. 16:24):

   a. We are joined into one by our spirit (with our mind, will, and emotion) cooperating with the crossing Spirit; whenever our spirit is one with the crossing Spirit, we experience the uniting Spirit.

   b. The initial Spirit must become the uniting Spirit within us; then we will have the oneness and the building and will be safeguarded from dissension and division.

Morning Nourishment

John   ...Holy Father, keep them in Your name, which You
17:11   have given to Me, that they may be one even as We are.
Exo.   And you shall make the boards for the tabernacle of
26:15   acacia wood, standing up.
    29 And you shall overlay the boards with gold, and
        make their rings of gold as holders for the bars; and
        you shall overlay the bars with gold.
Eph.   ...In Him also believing, you were sealed with the
1:13   Holy Spirit of the promise.

First, [the genuine oneness of the Body] was something in
the Lord's desire. This desire of the Lord's became His aspiration, and this aspiration was expressed in the prayer offered by
the Lord in John 17 (vv. 2, 6, 11, 14-24). The subject of the Lord's
prayer in John 17 is oneness. The Lord uttered this prayer out of
the divine aspiration. At that time this oneness was not yet a reality; however, a model of this oneness—the oneness among the
three of the Divine Trinity—was there. The Father and the Son
are one (vv. 11, 21), and this oneness implies or includes the
Spirit. In John 17 the Lord used the plural pronouns *We* (v. 11)
and *Us* (v. 21) to signify the Triune God. The Triune God is one,
and that oneness is a model of the oneness of the Body of Christ.
Because the oneness of the Body has the oneness among the
three of the Trinity as a model, John 17 tells us that this oneness
is altogether wrapped up with the Triune God (v. 21). The oneness of the Body of Christ is just the enlarged oneness of the Divine Trinity. The model was there at the time the Lord prayed,
but the enlargement was still to come. This enlarged oneness
came on the day of Pentecost. Through the outpouring of the
Spirit, the Body of Christ was produced (1 Cor. 12:13). That Body
is the solid oneness. (*The Intrinsic Problem in the Lord's Recovery Today and Its Scriptural Remedy,* pp. 10-11)

Today's Reading

The oneness mentioned by the Lord in His prayer in John 17
is mysterious, for it is a oneness realized and practiced in the

Triune God. Thank the Lord for the clear picture of this oneness in the building of the tabernacle in the Old Testament. The building of the tabernacle in Exodus corresponds to the oneness in John 17. The Lord prayed that all His believers would be one so that God could have a dwelling place on earth. The tabernacle was such a dwelling place. The oneness seen in the tabernacle is simply the building of the tabernacle.

The tabernacle had forty-eight boards. Because these boards were built together to be the dwelling place of God, the tabernacle is a clear picture of the oneness in the Triune God. This oneness is not in the acacia wood out of which the boards were made; it is in the gold that overlaid them. The wood and the gold signify the Christian's human and divine nature. The human nature is signified by the acacia wood, and the divine nature, by the gold. Each board was made of acacia wood overlaid with gold. Because we Christians are both wooden and golden, we are wonderful.

This oneness has three aspects. The first aspect, the initial aspect, is with the golden rings. I am quite certain that the golden rings were attached to the boards before the boards were overlaid with gold. Thus, the first step was to attach the rings to the boards and the second step was to overlay the boards with gold. The third step was to make the uniting bars, which held the forty-eight boards together and brought them into oneness. This oneness is the building, which is the dwelling place of God.

Sound Bible teachers and expositors agree that the rings signify the initial Spirit given to us, that is, the regenerating Spirit, the sealing Spirit mentioned in Ephesians 1. When we were regenerated, God put His Spirit into us. Immediately, the regenerating Spirit became the indwelling Spirit. This regenerating and indwelling Spirit is the initial Spirit given to us by God. (*Truth Messages,* pp. 103-104, 93-94)

Further Reading: The Intrinsic Problem in the Lord's Recovery
Today and Its Scriptural Remedy, ch. 1

Enlightenment and inspiration: _____

_____

_____

_____

Morning Nourishment

John
17:21-23
That they all may be one; even as You, Father, are in Me and I in You, that they also may be in Us; that the world may believe that You have sent Me. And the glory which You have given Me I have given to them, that they may be one, even as We are one; I in them, and You in Me, that they may be perfected into one...

After the golden rings were installed on the boards, the boards were overlaid with gold. The overlaying caused the golden rings and the overlaying gold to have one appearance. This indicates the spreading of the sealing Spirit, and it corresponds to our experience.

To have the rings without the overlaying gold is to be poor in gold. It is to have the Triune God as the rings but not as the gold overlaying the boards. To be in such a condition is to be poor in God. We need to learn to confess that we sometimes are poor in God. We may be rich in the self but quite poor in God. Therefore, we need the initial Spirit to spread throughout our being; that is, the initial gold must spread out in order to overlay us. As we grow in the Lord, the Spirit spreads within us and overlays us with Himself. (*Truth Messages,* pp. 95-96)

Today's Reading

To have simply the three rings is not to be rich in the expression of the proper oneness. Genuine oneness requires a full expression, a full appearance, of the gold. Therefore, day by day we need to be overlaid more with gold. The more the initial Spirit spreads within us, the more oneness we have. In addition to admitting that we are poor in God, we should also learn to confess that we are poor in the oneness. However, by the Lord's grace we can also say, "Hallelujah, I am rich in Christ, and I am also rich in the oneness!" When a board has been fully overlaid with gold, that is, with the Triune God, it is rich both in God and in the oneness.

If the gold had been taken away from the standing boards, leaving only the acacia wood, the boards would immediately have fallen down. Even if they had remained upright, standing side by side, they would still not have been one. Rather, they would have

been forty-eight separate, individual boards. Their oneness was
not in the acacia wood; it was in the gold. This clearly portrays the
fact that our oneness is not in humanity, but in divinity, in the Triune God. If the divine nature were taken away from us, we would
immediately become detached from one another. Although we
might still love one another,…we nevertheless would not be one.
The oneness of the standing boards of the tabernacle, or this oneness in the gold, symbolizes our oneness in the Triune God.

The gold was not only the oneness of the standing boards; it
was also their glory. By being overlaid with gold, the standing
boards bore the glory of the gold, for the shining of the gold was
their glory, their expression. Anyone who entered into the tabernacle could see on every hand the shining of the gold. Hence, the
oneness of the forty-eight boards was not only in the gold, signifying God, but also in the shining of the gold, signifying the glory of
God. In the same principle, our oneness today is in the Triune God
and in His glory, His shining.

Although we all are boards, we may be overlaid with a very thin
layer of gold. Yes, we may be in the Triune God, but we may not be
deeply in Him. Instead of being overlaid with gold, we may merely
be gilded with gold, like Babylon the Great in Revelation 17. If the
standing boards had been only gilded with gold, there would have
been no gold for the rings that supported the weight of the boards.
In order for the forty-eight heavy boards to be held together, they
each had to be overlaid with a heavy layer of gold.

In no other portion of the Bible is the Triune God revealed in
such a practical way as in chapter seventeen of John. The various
pronouns used—I, Us, You—indicate that the Triune God is related to our oneness. It is in the Triune God that we are perfected
into one. To be perfected means to have more gold. Only when the
boards were adequately overlaid with gold were they perfected
into one. This indicates that to be perfected into one means to gain
more of God. (*Truth Messages,* pp. 96-97, 84-85, 88)

Further Reading: Truth Messages, chs. 9-10

Enlightenment and inspiration: _____

_____

_____

_____

Morning Nourishment

Col. ...The Head, out from whom all the Body...grows
2:19 with the growth of God.
Phil. ...Christ Jesus my Lord, on account of whom I have
3:8-10 suffered the loss of all things and count *them* as refuse
that I may gain Christ and be found in Him...to know
Him and the power of His resurrection and the fellowship of His sufferings, being conformed to His death.

Oneness is not a superficial matter. It is a matter of sinking
deeply into the Triune God until we are fully overlaid with gold.
We all need a great deal more of God. It is not sufficient simply to
be coated with a thin layer of Him. If we truly have light on our
need to be overlaid with gold, we shall repent and say, "Lord, I repent that I am only gilded with gold. I have not yet been overlaid.
What I have experienced of You is merely gilding. It is good for
causing others to praise me, but it is not good for the real oneness,
for holding me together with others. When even a small problem
arises, my layer of gold is not sufficient, and the oneness is damaged. Lord, for the oneness, overlay me with an adequate amount
of gold." (*Truth Messages*, p. 88)

Today's Reading

The more we are overlaid with gold, the more oneness we
have. Nothing can damage the oneness that comes from our being
overlaid with an ample quantity of gold. The more we have of
God, the stronger is our oneness.

Recently, some among us became dissenting, although they
claimed to have seen the ground and to be for the Lord's recovery.
Because they had not been solidly overlaid with gold, they caused
the oneness to be damaged. The same thing may happen in the
future to anyone who is not fully overlaid with gold. Not having
an adequate amount of God can create a serious problem with the
oneness. The Lord's recovery is not a movement. We do not desire
to gain a large number of people. In the recovery we are concerned
for the genuine weight of gold. The important question is this:
How much of God do you have? The Lord's recovery consists of

God overlaying His recovered people with Himself.

Whenever I see that any are dissenting, I feel sorry for them. At the same time I realize that such a situation of dissension is a test, an exposure, and a purification. It is a test of what is real, of how much gold we actually have. We all need to gain more gold. It is not sufficient only to have a good heart, to know the truth, and to care for the Lord's recovery. Everything depends upon how much gold we have. We all can become dissenting if we are short of gold. This should be a warning to us all. Again I say that genuine oneness is possible only in the Triune God.

If we seriously consider the picture of the standing boards in Exodus 26, we shall be deeply impressed with how much we are short of God. From 1925, I began to read articles in Christian magazines about the overcoming life. Although these articles provided help on how to be victorious, they did not say that we needed more of God. We do not need to learn so many methods. Our need is simply to sink into the Triune God and to gain more of Him. God is our truth, our way, our life, our everything. If we do not have God, we have nothing. Our problem is that we are short of God, and our need is to gain more of Him.

If we do not gain the necessary gold, sooner or later we shall have a problem. We need the solid oneness. This oneness is the adequate amount of God we have obtained. Do not rely on teachings or doctrines. Moreover, do not depend on your own love or your natural affection. Not even your steady will is trustworthy in keeping the oneness. Only one thing is dependable for oneness, and that is the adequate amount of God. Just as the standing boards could be one only in the gold, we can be one only by sinking into God.

Today the Lord needs the genuine oneness. If we do not have this oneness, we cannot go on in the recovery. Hence, the most vital and crucial matter is the genuine oneness. The only way to be kept in this solid, real oneness is to have an adequate amount of the experienced God. This is our need today. (*Truth Messages,* pp. 88-90)

Further Reading: Truth Messages, ch. 9

Enlightenment and inspiration: _____

_____

_____

_____

Morning Nourishment

2 Cor. But we all with unveiled face, beholding and re-
3:18 flecting like a mirror the glory of the Lord, are being transformed into the same image from glory to
glory, even as from the Lord Spirit.

Rom. That the righteous requirement of the law might
8:4 be fulfilled in us, who do not walk according to the
flesh but according to the spirit.

We have seen that the gold overlays acacia wood. It will never
be applied to any other type of wood. This indicates that if our natural man has not been transformed, the Triune God will not overlay us. The Triune God will never overlay the flesh or the natural
man. The overlaying requires transformation. This is a crucial
matter.

Oneness requires transformation....If we are not transformed, we cannot be covered with the overlaying gold. I have no
doubt that you all have the three rings, the Triune God as the initial Spirit sealing you, giving you the sense of discernment and
enabling you to express the Lord whom you love. But I am concerned that day after day may go by without you allowing the
Lord to transform you. The Lord's overlaying us with Himself always goes along with transformation. Transformation may be
likened to railroad tracks, and the overlaying to the train that
moves on this track. If no track has been laid, it will be impossible
for the train to move. A particular part of our being cannot be
reached by the overlaying gold until that part of us has truly been
transformed. This should not be a mere doctrine to us. We need to
love the Lord, contact Him, get into His Word, pray, and walk
according to the spirit. If we do these things, transformation will
take place spontaneously. (*Truth Messages,* pp. 97, 99-100)

Today's Reading

I have been greatly exercised before the Lord in an attempt to
understand the [rebellious] situation. Gradually, the Lord showed
me that certain dear ones had nothing more than the three rings.
With them, there was no spreading of the gold because there was

no transformation. The reason there was no transformation was that in the experience of these dissenting ones there was no dealing of the cross....The standing boards are crossed by the uniting bars. This indicates that although we may be standing upright, the uniting Spirit crosses us....Without the cross there can be no resurrection. The cross is very positive because it ushers us into resurrection. It is in resurrection that our natural life is transformed. This transformation in resurrection brings in the overlaying gold.

Only when we all have been transformed and overlaid with gold will it no longer be possible for there to be dissension among us. Until we are thus transformed and overlaid, we shall always be in danger of falling into dissension. The only safeguard is to be overlaid with gold. We must not go on according to the natural being; instead of a natural humanity we must have a transformed humanity with the very humanity of Jesus as its element....Only the humanity of Jesus, which is a humanity in resurrection, is qualified to be overlaid with gold.

I beg you to bring this matter to the Lord in prayer. We need much prayer in order to realize that the steps to the genuine oneness come from our experience of God. Do not think that simply by reading this message you have the reality of what it is talking about. In order to have the reality of this word, we need time and much prayer. The realization of oneness is not easy because it is a divine reality. The divine nature must be wrought into our being. The initial Spirit, the Triune God installed in us as the rings, must spread throughout our being. This spreading requires transformation, and transformation demands that we take Christ as our life by loving Him, contacting Him, listening to His word, praying to Him, and walking in the spirit. If this is our experience, we shall be transformed and overlaid with gold. Then the oneness will be completed within us, and we shall be safeguarded from dissension and division. (*Truth Messages,* pp. 100-101)

Further Reading: Truth Messages, ch. 10

Enlightenment and inspiration: _____

_____

_____

_____

Morning Nourishment

Exo. **And you shall make bars of acacia wood, five for the**
26:26-28 **boards of the one side of the tabernacle, and five bars**
for the boards of the other side of the tabernacle, and
five bars for the boards of the side of the tabernacle at
the rear westward. And the middle bar shall pass
through in the center of the boards from end to end.
Rom. **The Spirit Himself witnesses with our spirit that we**
8:16 **are children of God.**

Although we may have the initial Spirit and some experience
of being overlaid with gold, we still need to go on to the uniting
Spirit. After the boards, the rings, and the overlaying gold, we
still need the bars. Without the bars, the forty-eight boards cannot be one, for it is the bars that hold them together. What do the
bars signify? Since we are the boards, the bars cannot represent
us. Furthermore, the rings signify the Triune God, and the gold
covering the boards signifies the spreading of God. Just as the
rings are a symbol of the initial Spirit, the bars are a symbol of
the uniting Spirit. The boards stand upright, and the bars unite
them by crossing them horizontally. (*Truth Messages*, p. 106)

Today's Reading

The uniting bars are not the Holy Spirit alone, but the Holy
Spirit with the human spirit. In the Epistles it is often difficult to
decide whether the Greek word for *spirit* should be rendered with
a capital letter or a lower case letter. In other words, it is difficult
to determine whether the Greek word refers to the Holy Spirit or
to the human spirit. Often it denotes the mingled spirit, the Holy
Spirit mingled with our spirit. Therefore, the uniting bars are not
only the Triune God added to man to bear responsibility; the
Spirit represented by these bars also includes the human spirit.
This means that if our spirit does not cooperate with the uniting
Spirit, the oneness cannot be realized in a practical way. The uniting Spirit is actually the mingled spirit. In this mingled spirit
there is both divinity and humanity, both gold and acacia wood.

Whether or not the uniting Spirit can actually join us into

one depends on whether or not we are willing to cooperate with this Spirit. If the Spirit does not have a way to pass through us, there can be no oneness. In order for the uniting Spirit to pass through us and thus join us with others, we need to receive the cross, for the uniting Spirit always crosses the standing boards. If we are willing to receive the cross, our spirit will cooperate with the uniting Spirit. Then the Spirit with our spirit will join us to another believer in Christ. We are joined into one by our spirit cooperating with the crossing Spirit. However, most of the time we are not willing to be crossed by the Spirit.

The uniting Spirit is seeking to cross through us to others. The question is whether or not we are willing to go along with Him. Whenever our spirit is one with the crossing Spirit, we experience the uniting Spirit. Every time we walk according to the Spirit, we experience the crossing of the Spirit. We stand, but we are crossed by the Spirit. The Spirit will never cross through us unless our spirit goes along with Him. When our spirit agrees with the crossing Spirit, we have the uniting bar. This is the unique way to keep the oneness. This understanding of the uniting bars is confirmed by our experience.

There are several steps to the oneness portrayed in the tabernacle. First, we have the initial Spirit, who is the regenerating and sealing Spirit. Then we have the process of transformation by which we are transformed into acacia wood. Along with transformation, there is the overlaying of the wood with the divine nature. Furthermore, the Spirit is continually endeavoring to cross us, to pass through us. In order for this to take place, our spirit, with our mind, will, and emotion, must go along with Him. Only then do we have the uniting bars, the five bars in three rows to unite the believers into one. When we have all these aspects, we have the oneness in the Triune God revealed in John 17. This means we have the building in the overlaying and uniting gold. (*Truth Messages,* pp. 108-109)

Further Reading: Truth Messages, chs. 10-11

Enlightenment and inspiration: _____

_____

_____

_____

Morning Nourishment

Eph.   With all lowliness and meekness, with long-suffering,
4:2-3   bearing one another in love, being diligent to keep
       the oneness of the Spirit in the uniting bond of peace.
Matt.   Then Jesus said to His disciples, If anyone wants to
16:24   come after Me, let him deny himself and take up his
       cross and follow Me.

We need to emphasize the importance of being crossed by the
uniting Spirit. The uniting Spirit not only strengthens us in
standing; it also crosses us. Something passes through us not ver-
tically but horizontally. Although we are standing, we still need to
be crossed. The standing Spirit must also be the crossing Spirit. If
we are willing to be crossed, it means that our spirit goes along
with the crossing Spirit. The Spirit will never join us to others
without this willingness. The uniting Spirit cannot unite me to
you unless your spirit is willing to cooperate with the Spirit.
When the uniting Spirit comes to me, it comes with the spirit of
another brother, and when it goes from me to still another, it goes
with my spirit. The uniting Spirit cannot unite us Himself. He
must have the cooperation of our spirit. This means that we must
be willing to be crossed by Him. (*Truth Messages,* pp. 109-110)

Today's Reading

If we see this matter, then we shall realize why, even after
more than nineteen centuries, the oneness for which the Lord
prayed in John 17 has not yet come into existence. Among today's Christians there is little transformation or overlaying with
the divine nature. Furthermore, there is little crossing of the
Spirit and little cooperation of the human spirit with the divine
Spirit. Hence, there is no oneness. But what about the situation
among us in the Lord's recovery? We need to ask ourselves how
much we have of transformation, the overlaying with the divine
nature, the crossing of the uniting Spirit, and the cooperation of
our spirit with the uniting Spirit. Are you willing to allow the
Spirit to cross through you? Yes, you may be standing firmly for
the Lord's testimony as one of the boards, but are you willing to

be crossed by the Spirit? Can the Spirit pass through you? Many times the Spirit cannot pass through us because we are not willing to be crossed by Him. Is your spirit willing to go with the Spirit to another saint? Please do not think that the Spirit of God Himself alone can unite us. No, He needs our spirit to go along with Him. This is the meaning of keeping the oneness of the Spirit with all lowliness, meekness, long-suffering, and with bearing one another in love.

As believers in Christ, we all have the initial Spirit. We are also undergoing the process of transformation and of being overlaid with the divine nature. But I am concerned that when the crossing Spirit comes to us, many are not willing for Him to cross through. We need to say, "Lord, my spirit is willing to go along with You. I am willing for You to cross through me." If you have this willingness, you will immediately and spontaneously have the uniting bars, and you will experience the practical oneness. The Holy Spirit with your spirit will pass on to the spirit of another saint. This will in turn help other brothers and sisters to be willing for the uniting Spirit to cross them.

The uniting Spirit crosses through all the members of the Body when the spirits of the members are willing to be crossed by Him. Through this willingness and this crossing we have the oneness. It was in this way that the entire tabernacle was brought into one. This is the oneness for the building, the dwelling place of God.

If you consider the picture of the tabernacle in the light of John 17, you will see the truth concerning oneness. To have such a oneness, we need the initial Spirit, we need the transformation into acacia wood, we need the overlaying with gold, and we need the crossing of the uniting Spirit according to the willingness of our spirit to cooperate with Him. Then we shall have the oneness and the building. This building is God's dwelling place with man on earth. (*Truth Messages*, pp. 110-112)

Further Reading: Truth Messages, ch. 11

Enlightenment and inspiration: _____

_____

_____

_____

Hymns, #1081

1   Father God, Thou art the source of life.
    We, Thy sons, are Thine expression;
    In Thy name, our dear possession.
    Father God, Thou art the source of life.

    In Thy life, in Thy life,
    We have oneness in Thy life.
    In Thy life, in Thy life,
    In Thy life, O Father, we are one.

2   How we thank Thee that Thy holy Word
    With Thy nature, saturates us;
    From the world it separates us.
    Thank Thee, Father, for Thy holy Word.

    Through Thy Word, through Thy Word,
    We have oneness through Thy Word.
    Through Thy Word, through Thy Word,
    Through Thy holy Word we're all made one.

3   Oh, the glory of the Triune God!
    We're His sons, oh, what a blessing!
    We His glory are expressing—
    Oh, the glory of the Triune God!

    In Thy glory, in Thy glory,
    In Thy glory we are one.
    In Thy glory, in Thy glory,
    In Thy glory we are all made one!

Composition for prophecy with main point and sub-points: _____

_____

_____

_____

_____

_____

_____

_____

_____

_____

_____

_____

_____

_____

_____

_____

_____

_____

_____

_____

_____

_____

_____

_____

_____

_____

_____

_____

_____

_____

_____

_____

_____

_____

_____

_____

The Vision and Practice
of the Genuine One Accord

Scripture Reading: John 17:11, 21-23; Eph. 4:3-6; Acts 1:14; 2:46; Rom. 15:5-6; 1 Cor. 1:10

Day 1
I. **The genuine one accord in the church is the practice of the oneness of the Body, which is the oneness of the Spirit (Eph. 4:3-6):**
   A. From Ephesians 4:4-6 we can see that our practice of the oneness is based upon the attribute of the oneness of the church: one Spirit, one Lord, one God, one Body, one faith, one baptism, one hope.
   B. The practice of the genuine one accord in the church is the application of the oneness (Acts 1:14; 2:46).
   C. The practice of the oneness is with the one accord; when the oneness is practiced, it becomes the one accord:
      1. In John the Lord emphasized oneness, but in Acts the one accord is emphasized (John 10:30; 17:11, 21-23; Acts 1:14; 2:46; 4:24; 15:25).

Day 2
&
Day 3
      2. The landmark that divides the Gospels and the Acts is the one accord among the one hundred and twenty (1:14):
         a. They had become one in the Body, and in that oneness they continued steadfastly with one accord in prayer (Eph. 4:3-6; Acts 1:14).
         b. When the apostles and the believers practiced the church life, they practiced it in one accord (2:46; 4:24; 5:12).
      3. The one accord is the heart, the kernel, the nucleus, of the oneness.
   D. Our not being in one accord means that we do not practice the Body:
      1. According to the proper interpretation of

the New Testament, the one accord is the
Body (Rom. 12:4-5; 15:5-6).

2. We must practice the principle of the Body;
then we will have the one accord (1 Cor.
12:12-13, 20, 27; 1:10).

E. We are for the one accord, but we are not for uni-
formity (1 John 2:12-14).

II. **The one accord refers to the harmony in
our inner being, in our mind and will (Acts
1:14):**

A. In Acts 1:14 the Greek word *homothumadon* is
used for one accord:

1. The word denotes a harmony of inward feeling in one's entire being.

2. We should be in the same mind and the
same will with the same purpose around
and within our soul and heart; this means
that our entire being is involved.

B. In Matthew 18:19 the Greek word *sumphoneo* is
used to signify the one accord:

1. The word means "to be in harmony, or accord" and refers to the harmonious sound of
musical instruments or voices.

2. The one accord, or the harmony of inward
feeling among the believers, is like a harmonious melody.

3. When we have the one accord, we become a
melody to God; we become a poem not
merely in writing but in sound, in voice, in
melody.

Day 4 III. **Today we can be in one accord because we
have one, all-inclusive vision—the vision of
the age (Prov. 29:18a; Acts 26:19):**

A. Many love God and serve Him, but everyone has
his own vision; as a result, there is no way to
have the one accord.

B. As long as we have different views on a minor
point, we cannot have the one accord (Phil.
3:15).

C. The vision that the Lord has given His recovery
is an all-inclusive vision—the ultimate consummation of all the visions in the Bible (Rev. 21:2,
10-11).

IV. **The teaching of the apostles is the holding
factor of the one accord (Acts 2:42, 46):**

A. The practice of the oneness—the one accord—is
according to the apostles' teaching (v. 42).

B. Acts tells us that there was one accord among
the believers and that all those who were in one
accord continued steadfastly in the apostles'
teaching.

C. The apostles taught the same thing to all the
saints in all the places and in all the churches
(1 Cor. 4:17; 7:17; 11:16; 14:33b-34):

1. We must also teach the same thing in all
the churches in every country throughout
the earth (Matt. 28:19-20).

2. There is no thought in the New Testament
that a teaching is good for one church but
not for the other churches; rather, the New
Testament reveals that all the churches
were the same in receiving the teachings
(Titus 1:9).

Day 5   V. **When we practice the one accord, we must
learn to be in one spirit with one soul (Phil.
1:27):**

A. We need to turn to our spirit and then enter into
our soul with one spirit that we may be in one
accord (2:2, 5; 4:2).

B. To practice the one accord, we should be attuned
in the same mind and in the same opinion; this
is to be one in our soul (1 Cor. 1:10).

C. To be in one accord is to be one in our whole being, and this results in our being one in our outward speaking (Rom. 15:5-6):

1. To have one mind and one mouth means
that we have only one Head—Christ—because only the Head has a mind and mouth;

we should think with the mind of Christ
and speak with the mouth of the Head (Col.
1:18a; Phil. 2:2, 5; 4:2).

2. Whenever we are in one accord, we speak
the same thing; we speak with one mouth.

3. The only way to be with one accord and one
mouth is to allow Christ the room to be
everything in our heart and in our mouth
that God may be glorified (Eph. 3:17a, 21).

Day 6   VI. **We should all have one heart and one way;
this one heart and one way is the one accord
(Jer. 32:39).**

VII. **If we have only one "scale," we will be fair,
just, and righteous, even as God is, and we
will keep the oneness and one accord in the
church (Deut. 25:13-16).**

VIII. **The one accord is the master key to every
blessing in the New Testament (Eph. 1:3;
Psa. 133).**

Morning Nourishment

Eph. Being diligent to keep the oneness of the Spirit in the
4:3-4 uniting bond of peace: One Body and one Spirit...
John And the glory which You have given Me I have given
17:22-23 to them, that they may be one, even as We are one; I
in them, and You in Me, that they may be perfected
into one...
Acts And when they heard *this*, they lifted up *their* voice
4:24 with one accord to God...

In the Body we need oneness; in the churches and among the churches, we need the one accord. The one accord is for our practice; the oneness is primarily for the actuality, for the fact....If we have only the oneness as an actuality, and do not have the present, practical one accord, the oneness that we have will be objective and abstract; it will not be real to us. If we would apply the oneness accomplished by the outpouring of the Spirit, we must practice the one accord. If among us there is no one accord, how could we say that there is oneness? If in a prayer meeting we each pray in our own way, without any accord among us, how could we say that we are practicing the oneness? As long as we have differences existing among us, the oneness is not applied. We must have the one accord to swallow up all the differences; then oneness will be present. (*The Intrinsic Problem in the Lord's Recovery Today and Its Scriptural Remedy*, pp. 23-24)

Today's Reading

The practice of the proper one accord in the church is the application of the oneness. Although oneness and one accord seem to be synonymous, there is a difference between them. The Lord did not teach us concerning oneness. In John 17 He prayed for oneness, but in Matthew 18 He led us to practice the one accord. In Matthew 18:19 the Lord spoke of two praying together on earth in one accord. That was His leading, His training, and His directing us to pray in one accord. As a test of whether we are practicing the oneness or not, we may check to see whether there is one accord in our prayer meeting. When certain ones pray, we may shake our head as an indication of our displeasure, and when others pray, we may nod our head as an expression of our agreement. Such a shaking and nodding of our head is strong evidence that we do not practice oneness, because we do not have the one accord.

In a church meeting there may be people of different races and colors. Our one accord could never be based on the different races and colors. We practice one accord based on the fact that we all have a common life. We may be different in race and in the color of our skin, but when we come together to pray, we must forget about the different races and colors. We do have a base for our oneness; thus, we can practice the one accord.

Not only so, if we do not have the same understanding, the same intention, the same purpose, the same goal, it will be impossible to pray together in one accord. There will be no base for such prayer. If we each have our own opinion, our own intention, and our own goal, there will be no base on which we can pray in one accord. But when we who are saved and who love the Lord and mean business for the Lord's purpose come together, we surely have the base to pray in one accord.

In John 17 the Lord Jesus prayed for the oneness of His believers. That oneness was only in His aspiration. A little more than fifty days later, on the day of Pentecost, the oneness in the Lord's aspiration was accomplished. The oneness in the Lord's aspiration became the oneness in actuality. This oneness is called "the oneness of the Spirit" (Eph. 4:3), the Spirit here being the consummated Spirit, the all-inclusive Spirit, as the consummation of the entire Triune God. We, the saved ones, possess this oneness as our heritage. We possess this oneness, we enjoy it, and we apply it. To apply this oneness is to keep it, and to keep it is to practice one accord. (*The Intrinsic Problem in the Lord's Recovery Today and Its Scriptural Remedy,* pp. 24-25)

Further Reading: The Intrinsic Problem in the Lord's Recovery Today and Its Scriptural Remedy, chs. 1-2

Enlightenment and inspiration: _____

_____

_____

_____

Morning Nourishment

Acts These all continued steadfastly with one accord in
1:14 prayer...
1 Cor. For also in one Spirit we were all baptized into one
12:13 Body, whether Jews or Greeks, whether slaves or
free, and were all given to drink one Spirit.
20 But now the members are many, but the body one.
27 Now you are the Body of Christ, and members individually.

We must realize that the practices in the Lord's recovery are
not matters for others to copy. You must have the life. To do anything you need the life. You have to see what the landmark was
of the one hundred twenty in the book of Acts. The landmark
that divides the Gospels and the Acts was not the baptism in the
Holy Spirit. The landmark was the one accord of the one hundred twenty. If you want to experience the baptism in the Spirit,
you must have the one accord. If all the members of a local
church have the one accord, the baptism in the Spirit will be
there. If you really want to practice the proper way to preach the
gospel, you need the one accord. Without this key, no door can be
opened. The one accord is the "master key to all the rooms," the
master key to every blessing in the New Testament.

For us to be in the same one spirit with the same one soul, one
mind, and one will is to have the one accord, which is the key to
all the New Testament blessings and bequests. Otherwise, we
will repeat the pitiful history of Christianity by being another
group of Christians repeating the same kind of disaccord. (*Elders' Training, Book 7: One Accord for the Lord's Move*, pp. 19-20)

Today's Reading

The impact is with the one accord, and the one accord actually is the blending. If we do not have the one accord, God cannot
answer our prayer, because we do not practice the Body. Our not
being in one accord means that we do not practice the Body. According to the proper interpretation of the New Testament, the
one accord is the one Body. We must practice the principle of the

Body; then we will have the one accord. Although we may not fight with one another, we still may not have the one accord. Because we have remained together, we have seen the Lord's blessing, but only in a limited way. Therefore, we need to have the one accord to practice the Body.

Today we desire to be blended, and our being blended will surely produce a one accord in our spirit under the direction of the Spirit. In Matthew 18:19 the Lord spoke of two praying together on earth in harmony. In the book of Acts, we can see that the one hundred twenty practiced the Lord's command to pray in harmony, to pray in one accord (1:14). Their one accord was produced by their being in the spirit.

By reading the New Testament we can see the difference between what the disciples were in the Gospels and what they were in Acts....How could the one hundred twenty pray together for ten days in one accord? Only people who are in the spirit could do this. They were people in the spirit because the Spirit had been breathed into them....They prayed in one accord, and they prayed to build up the one accord. There was a very strong one accord among them.

We cannot say that there is no one accord among us today. To say this is not fair. We do have the one accord, but everything has its degree....We have the one accord today, but how high and how deep is our one accord? This is a problem. The one hundred twenty prayed in one accord for ten days. Probably on the tenth day, their one accord went to the heavens. It became the strongest and the highest one accord. At that time the heaven opened and the Spirit was poured out. (*Fellowship concerning the Urgent Need of the Vital Groups,* pp. 88, 104-106)

Further Reading: Elders' Training, Book 7: One Accord for the Lord's Move, chs. 1-5, 8; *Fellowship concerning the Urgent Need of the Vital Groups,* msgs. 7, 9-10, 12; *Elders' Training, Book 9: The Eldership and the God-ordained Way (1),* ch. 1; *The Governing and Controlling Vision in the Bible,* ch. 2

Enlightenment and inspiration: _____

_____

_____

_____

Morning Nourishment

Acts
1:14   These all continued steadfastly with one accord in prayer...

15:25   It seemed good to us, having become of one accord, to choose men to send to you together with our beloved Barnabas and Paul.

Matt.
18:19   Again, truly I say to you that if two of you are in harmony on earth concerning any matter for which they ask, it will be done for them from My Father who is in the heavens.

[In Acts 1:14] the word in Greek for "one accord," *homothumadon,* is strong and all-inclusive. *Homo* means "the same" and *thumos* means "mind, will, purpose (soul, heart)."...In the book of Acts the one hundred twenty prayed together in one mind, in the same mind, in the same will with the same purpose around and within the soul and the heart. Whenever we pray, we surely should exercise our spirit, but we also should be in the same mind and the same will with the same purpose around and within our soul and heart. This means that our entire being is involved. After the Lord's ascension, the one hundred twenty became the kind of persons who were in one mind, in one will, with one purpose around their soul and heart. For them to be in one accord meant that their entire beings were one. No other book of the Bible uses the word for "one accord" as much as Acts.

The one accord is the key and the life pulse of prayer, the Spirit, and the Word. You may pray much, seek the baptism of the Holy Spirit, and acquire a lot of knowledge from the Word, yet if you are short of the one accord you cannot see the blessing. (*Elders' Training, Book 7: One Accord for the Lord's Move,* pp. 10-11)

Today's Reading

In Matthew 18:19 the Greek word *sumphoneo* is used....It means "to be in harmony, or accord" and refers to the harmonious sound of musical instruments or voices. Eventually,...our one accord must be like a harmonious melody. Such a one accord is the nucleus of the oneness.

If among those in a group there is no one accord, what can the Lord do with them? This is why my burden concerning the vital groups is so heavy. I am very clear that we do not have the full and complete one accord among us. Therefore, in a sense it is hard for the Lord to move freely among us. If we are not in one accord, God has no way to answer our prayer. If God does not have a way to answer our prayer, what can He do with us? Without the one accord, it is difficult to get people saved, converted, and regenerated by the dynamic salvation of God. Thus, our inadequacy in the one accord is a sickness that is more than serious. We have been sick for years, yet we might have been unconscious of our sickness. We may come to the meetings, praise the Lord, and prophesy, but we may do all these things without being conscious of the fact that we do not have the adequate one accord.

Although I have studied the Bible for many years, I did not see until recently that oneness is like the body, and one accord is like the heart within the body. Our sickness is not just like a sickness in the outward, physical body; our sickness is like a sickness in the heart within the body. I am speaking the truth frankly and honestly, according to what the Lord has shown me and according to my pure conscience. We need to know what our sickness is. The sickness among us is that we do not have the one accord adequately. Therefore, we maintain only a oneness with a sick "heart." In these past four or five years even this unhealthy oneness has been broken by the dissenting ones. They would not even care for the oneness. We are still here for the oneness, yet within us there is an inadequacy in the one accord. Because of this, it is hard for the Lord to answer our prayer, especially in the matter of fruit-bearing for the increase of the Lord's recovery. For this, surely we need to humble ourselves before Him. (*Fellowship concerning the Urgent Need of the Vital Groups,* pp. 76, 77-78)

Further Reading: Elders' Training, Book 7: One Accord for the Lord's Move, chs. 1-5, 8; Fellowship concerning the Urgent Need of the Vital Groups, msgs. 7, 9-10, 12

Enlightenment and inspiration: _____

_____

_____

Morning Nourishment

Prov. Where there is no vision, the people cast off re-
29:18 straint...

Acts Therefore, King Agrippa, I was not disobedient to
26:19 the heavenly vision.

Phil. Let us therefore, as many as are full-grown, have
3:15 this mind; and if in anything you are otherwise
minded, this also God will reveal to you.

Acts And they continued steadfastly in the teaching
2:42 and the fellowship of the apostles, in the breaking
of bread and the prayers.

46 And day by day, continuing steadfastly with one
accord in the temple and breaking bread from
house to house...

Where there is no vision, the people cast off restraint, because there is no one accord. It is true that many people love the
Lord and serve God, but everyone has his opinion and his own
vision. As a result, there is no way to have the one accord. This is
why Christianity has become so weak. God's people are divided
and split apart. There are divisions everywhere.

Today we can be in one accord because we have only one vision and one view. We are all in this up-to-date, all-inheriting
vision. We have only one viewpoint. We speak the same thing
with one heart, one mouth, one voice, and one tone, serving the
Lord together. The result is a power that will become our strong
morale and our impact. This is our strength. Once the Lord's recovery possesses this power, there will be the glory of increase
and multiplication. Today our situation is not yet to that point; it
is not yet at the peak. Although we do not have many major con-
tentions, we do have some small complaints and criticisms.
These things lower our morale. (*The Vision of the Age*, pp. 53-54)

Today's Reading

Recently I have felt the importance of the one accord. As long
as we have different views on a minor point, we cannot have the
one accord. This is why in this training, right from the start, I

spoke about the vision in the Lord's recovery. I believe [you] all...
love the Lord, and all of you want to be in one accord, but if our
vision is not up-to-date, it is impossible for us to be one.

What is our vision? Our vision is that God so loved the world
that He gave His Son to die for us to redeem us, the sinners, in
order that we can have the life of Christ and be regenerated by
Him to be God's children, enjoying the riches of the Triune God
to become the Body of Christ. In practice, the Body is expressed
as the local churches in various localities, practicing the Body
life in a practical and proper way. This Body, the church of God, is
the focus of God's economy.

The vision that the Lord has given to His recovery is an
all-inclusive one. It includes the economy of God, the mingling
of God and man, the dispensing of the Divine Trinity, and the
believers' salvation in Christ, including God's selection, calling,
regeneration, sanctification, renewing, transformation, conformation, and glorification. In the history of the development of
Christian doctrine, this entire set of truths finds its full recovery
only among us. Such truths as selection, calling, regeneration,
sanctification, renewing, transformation, conformation, and glorification were not recovered much before us, and the recovery of
these truths will not increase much after us. This set of truths
has found its full recovery among us.

If we have different emphases and different ways of doing
things, our energy will be dissipated, and our faith will be weakened. We will lose the one accord, and our morale will be gone.
However, if we are in one accord and we preach the gospel desperately, we will become hotter and hotter; our mutual burning
will heighten our determination. Even the new ones will be
brought into the proper function. We will have an invincible
morale, and we will march over all obstacles. Wherever we go,
we will more than conquer. This is what we must have today.
(*The Vision of the Age,* pp. 70, 78-79, 86)

Further Reading: The Vision of the Age, chs. 2-3

Enlightenment and inspiration: _____

_____

_____

_____

Morning Nourishment

Phil. ...That you stand firm in one spirit, with one soul
1:27 striving together *along* with the faith of the gospel.
1 Cor. ...That you all speak the same thing and *that* there
1:10 be no divisions among you, but *that* you be attuned
in the same mind and in the same opinion.
Rom. Now the God of endurance and encouragement
15:5-6 grant you to be of the same mind toward one another according to Christ Jesus, that with one accord you may with one mouth glorify the God and
Father of our Lord Jesus Christ.

When we practice the one accord, we must learn to be in one spirit and with one soul (Phil. 1:27). We may be bodily sitting together in the same room, but if we are not one in our spirit, it is certain that we will not be one in our soul. To practice the one accord, we must learn to turn to our spirit and then to enter into our soul with the spirit that we may be in the one accord.

To practice the one accord, we must be attuned in the same mind and in the same opinion (1 Cor. 1:10). To be attuned in the same mind is to practically be one in our soul. When the thoughts in our mind are expressed in our speaking, they become our opinions. When the opinions remain in our mind, they are simply our thoughts. When our differences in thinking are expressed as opinions, that may cause a problem. (*The Intrinsic Problem in the Lord's Recovery Today and Its Scriptural Remedy,* p. 28)

Today's Reading

Although the church in Philippi was established in good order and had fellowship with Paul in the furtherance of the gospel, there was nevertheless dissension among them. By this we see that it is very difficult to avoid dissension. It can exist anywhere and at any time. The source of dissension is our opinions. Opinions come from the mind, the main part of the soul. In the book of Philippians Paul speaks often of the soul, the mind, and thinking. In 1:27 he uses the expression "with one soul," and in 2:2, the expression "joined in soul." In 2:20 he uses the term "like-souled."

We in the church life today need to be one in the soul. Christians frequently speak of being one in the Lord or one in the Spirit, but have you ever heard believers speak of being one in the soul? Until we are one in soul, there is no practicality to our oneness. Our oneness will be that of shaking hands over the fence. Christians talk about oneness, but they still hold to their dissenting opinions. Paul's concept of oneness was different. In Philippians he makes it clear that we need to be one in soul. In order to be one in soul, we need to be transformed and renewed in our mind. (*Life-study of Philippians,* p. 14)

Romans 15:6 tells us that we should be "with one accord" and "with one mouth." The word "accord" includes the mind, will, and purpose in the soul and the heart. We need to have one mind and one mouth. This means that we only have one Head because only the head has a mouth and a mind. We all take the Lord Jesus as the Head....If we considered this matter, we would not speak so loosely or freely; we would not speak whatever we like. You may like to speak something which the Head does not like....Your speaking interferes with or profanes the mouth of the Head.

What does it mean that we all have one mind and one mouth? This means "it is no longer I...but it is Christ who lives in me" (Gal. 2:20a). It is no more I, but Christ the Head who lives in me. He has a mouth, He has a mind, and I take Him as my person, so I would never use my mouth any longer to speak anything. Who could believe that so many millions of Christians with different languages could have one mouth? The Bible tells us this and we need to practice the one mouth to be one in speaking. (*Elders' Training, Book 7: One Accord for the Lord's Move,* pp. 47-48)

Further Reading: Life-study of Philippians, msgs. 2, 8; *Elders' Training, Book 7: One Accord for the Lord's Move,* chs. 1-5, 8; *Elders' Training, Book 10: The Eldership and the God-ordained Way (2),* ch. 4; *The Oneness and the One Accord according to the Lord's Aspiration and the Body Life and Service according to His Pleasure,* ch. 1; *Life-study of Romans,* msg. 29

Enlightenment and inspiration: _____

_____
_____
_____

Morning Nourishment

Jer. And I will give them one heart and one way, to fear
32:39 Me all the days, for their own good and for *the good
of* their children after them.
Deut. You shall not have in your bag differing weights,
25:13-15 one heavy and one light. You shall not have in your
house differing measures, one large and one small.
A full and righteous weight you shall have, *and* a
full and righteous measure you shall have, in order that your days may be extended upon the land
which Jehovah your God is giving you.

Deuteronomy 25:13-16 covers the judgment concerning
weights and measures...Those who have differing weights and
measures actually have differing scales. In the church life today, we may have differing scales—one scale for measuring
others and a different scale for measuring ourselves. Having
differing scales, we may condemn a certain thing in others but
justify the same thing in ourselves.

Although we should not have differing scales in the church
life, one scale for weighing ourselves and other scales for
weighing the brothers and sisters, we all have failed in this
matter. Not one of us is an exception. Using the language of ac-
counting, we may say that it is easy for us to "debit" others and
"credit" ourselves. Instead of doing this, we should give others
more credit and ourselves more debit.

I emphasize the practice of having differing scales because
this practice is a sickness, a disease, in the church life. This is
the source of disaccord. Instead of keeping the oneness and the
one accord, we have disaccord. May we all receive mercy from
the Lord to no longer have differing scales but, like our God, to
have the same scale for everyone. (*Life-study of Deuteronomy,*
pp. 134-136)

Today's Reading

We, the chosen people of God, should all have one heart and
one way [Jer. 32:39]. We should have one heart to love God, to

seek God, to live God, and to be constituted with God. This means that we love to be the expression of God. The one way is just the Triune God. The Lord Jesus said, "I am the way" (John 14:6a).

Christians today are divided because they take many different ways other than Christ. The Catholic Church has the Catholic way, and the Orthodox Church has the Orthodox way. Each denomination and independent group has its own way.

What should be our way in the Body of Christ? As the Body of Christ, we should take the way of the inner law, which is the Triune God with His divine capacity. We should all have one heart to love Him, and we should all take Him as our life and our way. This one heart and one way is the one accord (Acts 1:14). If we do not have one heart and one way, we cannot be in one accord.

For eternity in the New Jerusalem there will be only one way....In the middle of the street, the river of water of life flows, and in the river the tree of life grows. This indicates that the way, the life, and the life supply are all one. It also indicates what our way should be today. Our way in the Lord's recovery is life; it is the inner law of life; it is the very Triune God Himself.

I am sorry to say that in recent years there was a turmoil among us, and this turmoil brought in division. The reason for this turmoil was that certain ones wanted to take a way other than life, a way other than Christ, the Triune God, and the inner law. Divisions are always the result of taking a way other than Christ. If we keep ourselves to the one way, there will be no division. We praise the Lord that in His restoration He will give His people one heart to love Him and express Him and one way to enjoy Him. (*Life-study of Jeremiah,* pp. 188-190)

Further Reading: Life-study of Deuteronomy, msg. 19; *Life-study of Jeremiah,* msg. 27

Enlightenment and inspiration: _____

_____
_____
_____

Hymns, #779

1 Pray with one accord in spirit,
     Not according to our thought,
   But alone by the anointing,
     As the Lord has ever sought.

     Pray with one accord in spirit,
       Not according to our thought,
     But alone by the anointing,
       As the Lord has ever sought.

2 Pray with one accord in spirit,
     By the cross deny the soul;
   All desires and all intentions
     Let the Spirit now control.

3 Pray with one accord in spirit,
     Pray as in the heavenlies;
   All the earthly interests treading,
     Fight the principalities.

4 Pray with one accord in spirit,
     Supplicate relatedly;
   Seek the Lord, His mind, His leading,
     In the Spirit's harmony.

5 Pray with one accord in spirit,
     Pray and watch persistently;
   For God's kingdom and His glory,
     Pray and watch in harmony.

6 Pray with one accord in spirit
     Seeking God in unity;
   In the Spirit of the Body
     Ever pray in harmony.

Composition for prophecy with main point and
sub-points: _____

_____

_____

_____

_____

_____

_____

_____

_____

_____

_____

_____

_____

_____

_____

_____

_____

_____

_____

_____

_____

_____

_____

_____

_____

_____

_____

_____

_____

_____

_____

_____

_____

_____

The Unique Fellowship
in the Lord's Unique Recovery

Scripture Reading: Acts 2:42; 1 Cor. 1:9; 10:16; Phil. 2:1;
1 John 1:3, 7

Day 1   I. **We need to keep the unique fellowship in the Lord's unique recovery (Acts 2:42; 1 John 1:3):**
   A. The Lord's recovery is unique; there is not another recovery, just as there is not another Body of Christ or another New Testament.
   B. The fellowship of the apostles, which is the fellowship of the Body of Christ, is the fellowship for this unique recovery of the Lord (Acts 2:42).

   II. **Just as there is the circulation of blood in the human body, so there is a circulation in the Body of Christ—a circulation which the New Testament calls fellowship (1 John 1:3, 7):**
   A. Fellowship is a common participation, a joint participation; thus, to have fellowship is to have a corporate participation in something (Phil. 4:14; 2:1).
   B. Because the divine life is organic, rich, moving, and active, it has an issue, a certain kind of outcome; the issue, the outcome, of the divine life is the fellowship of life (1 John 1:1-3).

Day 2   C. In order to have the unique fellowship, we must live by and behave in the divine life, not in our natural life (Rom. 8:2, 6, 10-11).
   D. If we would live thoroughly in the divine fellowship, we need to experience the cross (Matt. 16:24).

Day 3   III. **Fellowship is related to oneness (1 Cor. 1:9;**
&   **6:17; 10:16-17; 12:20):**
Day 4   A. The fellowship, the circulation, of the divine life in the Body brings all the members of the Body into oneness (Eph. 4:3-6).
   B. This oneness is called the oneness of the Spirit (v. 3); it is also the oneness of the Body (v. 4; 1 Cor. 12:12-13).

C. As long as we have the divine life flowing within us, we are in this oneness—the oneness of the Body, the oneness among all the saints.

D. The unique fellowship is the genuine oneness of the Body of Christ as the unique ground for the believers to be kept one in Christ (Eph. 4:3-6).

IV. **The fellowship among the churches is the fellowship of the Body of Christ (1 Cor. 10:16):**

A. The Lord's recovery is based upon the truth that Christ has only one Body, which is expressed in many localities as the local churches (Eph. 1:22-23; 4:4; Rev. 1:11).

B. Because there is one Spirit, there is only one Body, and there is only one circulation of life in the Body; this circulation is the fellowship of the Body of Christ (Eph. 4:4; 1 John 1:3, 7).

C. The fellowship of the Body of Christ is the circulation, the current of *the* Spirit; when *the* Spirit is circulating within the Body of Christ, divinity, humanity, Christ's person, Christ's death, and Christ's resurrection all are circulating.

D. A local church is a part of the unique Body of Christ, and the fellowship of the Body is universally one; in fellowship there is no separation (Rev. 1:11; 2:7a):

1. No church or region should isolate itself from the fellowship of the Body.

2. The result of a church or a region isolating itself from the fellowship of the Body of Christ is darkness, confusion, division, and death.

E. Whenever we come to the Lord's table, we come to practice the fellowship of the Body (1 Cor. 10:16-17):

1. The Lord's table is a testimony that we who belong to Christ are one:

   a. We are one bread, one Body, because we all partake of one bread (v. 17).

   b. Our partaking of Christ constitutes us into His one Body.

2. If we isolate ourselves from the fellowship of the Body, we are not qualified to partake of the Lord's body, because the loaf on the table in the Lord's supper signifies the entire Body of Christ.

Day 5   F. Among all the churches that compose the one universal Body of Christ, there is no organization, but there is the fellowship of the Body of Christ (Phil. 1:5).

G. The divine fellowship is the reality of living in the Body of Christ (1 Cor. 1:9; 12:12-13, 27).

V. **The fellowship of the Body of Christ, which is the fellowship among the churches, is the fellowship of the apostles (Acts 2:42; 1 John 1:3):**

A. In the church life in the Lord's recovery, we follow and practice the fellowship of the apostles, which is based upon the teaching of the apostles (Acts 2:42):

1. Teaching creates fellowship, and fellowship comes from teaching (1 Cor. 4:17; 1:9; 10:16).

2. The teaching is the element and the realm of fellowship; the unique fellowship is produced by the unique teaching, the apostles' teaching.

3. If we teach wrongly or differently from the apostles' teaching, our teaching will produce a sectarian, divisive fellowship (1 Tim. 1:3-4; 6:3).

4. In the Lord's recovery today, we are under the apostles' teaching and in the apostles' fellowship (Acts 2:42).

5. In our work for the Lord, we must keep ourselves in the apostles' fellowship (1 Cor. 15:58; 16:10; Eph. 4:12).

Day 6   B. The circulation of the divine life among the believers through the apostles and from the Father is the fellowship of the Body, which comprises all the local churches (2 Cor. 13:14; 1 John 1:3, 7).

C. In the fellowship of the divine life, we join with

the apostles and the Triune God for the carrying
out of God's purpose (v. 3):

1. John's word concerning fellowship in 1 John
   1:3 indicates a putting away of private interests and a joining with others for a certain
   common purpose.

2. To have fellowship with the apostles, to be in
   the fellowship of the apostles, and to have
   fellowship with the Triune God in the apostles' fellowship is to put aside our private
   interests and join with the apostles and the
   Triune God for the carrying out of God's purpose.

D. We need to see and have the boldness to say that
   we are in the unique fellowship of the Lord's recovery, which is the recovered apostles' fellowship.

Morning Nourishment

Acts **And they continued steadfastly in the teaching**
2:42 **and the fellowship of the apostles...**
1 John **(And the life was manifested, and we have seen**
1:2-3 **and testify and report to you the eternal life, which**
was with the Father and was manifested to us);
that which we have seen and heard we report also
to you that you also may have fellowship with us,
and indeed our fellowship is with the Father and
with His Son Jesus Christ.

The fellowship of the divine life is the issue and flow of the divine life. Because the divine life is organic, rich, moving, and active, it has a particular issue, a certain kind of outcome. The issue, the outcome, of the divine life is the fellowship of life.

This fellowship is first mentioned in Acts 2:42....The fellowship of the apostles is the fellowship received by the apostles from the Triune God. According to 1 John 1:3,...this fellowship is from the Father and the Son to the apostles, and then from the apostles to all those who have received eternal life, the life of the Father. This means that the apostles receive the fellowship from the Father and transmit this fellowship to the believers by dispensing the divine life into them. Therefore, three parties are involved: the Father, the apostles, and the believers. Among these three parties something is circulating. This is the circulation of the divine life among the believers through the apostles and from the Father. This circulation is the fellowship of the Body, which comprises all the local churches. All the churches on earth are one Body, and within this Body there is the circulation of the divine life. In the New Testament this circulation of the divine life in the Body is called the fellowship. (*The Conclusion of the New Testament*, pp. 2177-2178)

Today's Reading

We always need to remember that we are in the Lord's recovery and that His recovery is unique. There is not another recovery, just as there is not another Body of Christ or another New Testament. The fellowship of the apostles is the fellowship for this unique

---

61 **WEEK 4 — DAY 1**

recovery of the Lord. When we see something going on in the recovery which is not so good, we need to have this kind of fellowship and a proper attitude....We should try the best to help the situation by fellowshipping so that it can be improved and corrected. If there is anything wrong, we can and should fellowship and pray together and seek the Lord's leading to improve the situation for the benefit of all the saints. This will be a real help to the Lord's recovery.

When I came into the recovery, I realized what the recovery was and that it was uniquely one. The one who brought the recovery to China among us was Brother Watchman Nee. If I would not have taken the way of the recovery, I could have had a work in northern China, but I gave that up. I fully realized that the Lord has only one Body, one work, one Bible, one revelation, and one current, one flow, in one fellowship. At that time Brother Nee was being used by the Lord. I never tried to speak anything different from his teaching. This does not mean that I did not have any other teachings, but my speaking always followed Brother Nee's speaking in order to keep the unique fellowship in the Lord's unique recovery. I felt that it was a glory to participate in the Lord's recovery in such a subjective way with Brother Nee. I thank the Lord that He had mercy upon me in helping me to have the best choice. In Moses' blessing in Deuteronomy 33, there is the term "the choicest things" (vv. 13-16). I realize that the Lord has been giving me the choicest things throughout my years in the recovery. This is due to His mercy in placing me and keeping me all the time in His recovery. As long as we are preserved in the Lord's way, we are preserved in the oneness in the unique fellowship. There is only one Lord, one Body, one Bible, one divine revelation, one speaking, one recovery, one fellowship, and one way to practice the recovery. (*A Brief Presentation of the Lord's Recovery*, pp. 39-40)

Further Reading: The Conclusion of the New Testament, msgs. 203-204; *A Brief Presentation of the Lord's Recovery*, "The Fellowship of the Churches in the Lord's Recovery"; *The Present Turmoil in the Lord's Recovery and the Direction of the Lord's Move Today*, ch. 1

Enlightenment and inspiration: _____

_____

_____

_____

Morning Nourishment

1 John If we say that we have fellowship with Him and yet
1:6-7 walk in the darkness, we lie and are not practicing
the truth; but if we walk in the light as He is in the
light, we have fellowship with one another, and the
blood of Jesus His Son cleanses us from every sin.

Phil. If there is therefore...any fellowship of spirit...
2:1

The apostles' fellowship is with the Father and the Son
(1 John 1:3) and is also the fellowship of the Spirit (2 Cor. 13:14),
which the apostles participated in and ministered to the believers through the preaching of the divine life (1 John 1:2-3).
Preaching produces fellowship, and fellowship must be of the divine life. The blood circulation in our physical body is crucial to
our staying alive. This blood circulation is the fellowship of our
physical life. If this fellowship is stopped, disease or death can
result....Today in the church, we must realize that if we are going to keep the proper fellowship, we must learn to live by the divine life. When we live by the divine life, we are in the circulation
of the divine life, the fellowship. (*The God-ordained Way to Practice the New Testament Economy*, pp. 155-156)

Today's Reading

Perhaps a certain brother has the burden to raise up the
church life in another locality. The leading brothers may come to
this brother to tell him that they need more fellowship. This
brother then may respond, "What is wrong with my going to another city? Why do you have to come to check on me?" If this
brother responds to the leading ones in this way, he is speaking
by his natural life and not by the divine life. He needs a change of
attitude. He should respond to the leading brothers from his
spirit by the divine life by saying, "Brothers, I am happy that you
want to have more fellowship with me. I also want to have more
fellowship with you to receive your help." When this brother responds in such a way, he is speaking in the spirit by the divine
life and conversing with the leading ones in the fellowship of the
apostles. To say things and behave by our own life is to get out of

the fellowship of the apostles. As long as we do things apart from the spirit and not with the divine life but with our natural life, we are outside of the fellowship of the apostles.

We need a vision of the apostles' teaching and fellowship to guide us, control us, and restrict us. "Where there is no vision, the people cast off restraint" (Prov. 29:18). Without such a vision, our work could issue in division. We should be in the teaching of the apostles and in the fellowship of the apostles....Our human life may be ethical, moral, and proper, but it is still our natural life. If we walk in our natural life, we are outside the fellowship of the apostles. Then we may set up another fellowship that will create a division. To keep the one way for the one goal and to stay in the fellowship of the apostles, we must live and behave in the divine life. When we live and behave in the divine life, we keep ourselves in the teaching and fellowship of the apostles, and in this fellowship we will have one way for one goal. Then we will keep the oneness in the Lord's Body.

The apostles' fellowship is the fellowship in which the believers enjoy the divine life and through which they fellowship with one another in the spirit (Phil. 2:1; Acts 2:42). In the fellowship of the apostles, there is the enjoyment of the divine life. This fellowship is altogether a matter of the divine life in the mingled spirit. We need to do everything in our spirit with the divine life. This unique fellowship is the genuine oneness of the Body of Christ as the unique ground for the believers to be kept one in Christ (Eph. 4:3-6). You may go to another locality and say, "We are going to take the standing of the church."...If you take the church ground by your natural life for your own standing, the ground on which you stand is the ground of division. The ground of the church must be the ground of oneness, and this oneness can only be kept by our being in the spirit with the divine life. (*The God-ordained Way to Practice the New Testament Economy,* pp. 156-157)

Further Reading: The God-ordained Way to Practice the New Testament Economy, ch. 17

Enlightenment and inspiration: _____

_____

_____

_____

Morning Nourishment

Eph. 4:3-4 Being diligent to keep the oneness of the Spirit in the uniting bond of peace: One Body and one Spirit, even as also you were called in one hope of your calling.

1 Cor. 12:12-13 For even as the body is one and has many members, yet all the members of the body, being many, are one body, so also is the Christ. For also in one Spirit we were all baptized into one Body...and were all given to drink one Spirit.

Fellowship is related to oneness. Just as the circulation of blood in the human body causes all the members of the body to be one, so the fellowship of the divine life in the Body of Christ causes the Body to be one. If any member of our physical body does not participate adequately in the circulation of blood in the body, that member will become unhealthy. The way to cure such a problem is to bring that member back into the circulation of the blood. The principle is the same with the fellowship of the Body of Christ. All those who believe in Christ Jesus,...have the divine life. This divine life has a circulation; that is, the divine life circulates within all of us. This circulation of the divine life in the Body brings all the members of the Body into oneness. This oneness is called the oneness of the Spirit; it is also the oneness of the Body. As long as we have the divine life flowing within us, we are in this oneness, the oneness of the Body, the oneness among all the saints. This oneness includes not only the believers but also the Triune God. This is the fellowship among the churches. (*The Conclusion of the New Testament*, p. 2178)

Today's Reading

If we realize what the fellowship among the churches is, we shall not have the concept that a local church should be altogether independent. In its local administration a local church is independent. However, according to the nature, essence, and intrinsic element of the church, no local church can be independent. To be independent is to be in darkness. Many Christian groups are in darkness because they have cut themselves off from the one, divine fellowship of the unique, divine life, the life of the Triune God.

It is possible that, among us in the Lord's recovery, certain churches or regions may make themselves independent. They may isolate themselves from the Body. They do not want to keep their church or their region open to the entire Body, that is, open to all the local churches on earth. As a result, to some extent at least, they cut themselves off from the fellowship among the churches. The result is darkness, confusion, division, and death. This should be a warning to us all....A church cannot be in a healthy condition if it isolates itself from the fellowship of the Body of Christ.

Although the administration of the church is separate and equal locally, the fellowship of the church is one universally. In fellowship there is no separation. On this entire earth there is only one fellowship, and this fellowship is universally one....There are separate churches in many cities, but there is only one fellowship in the entire universe.

In Ephesians 4:4...the Body is mentioned before the Spirit because the oneness among us is related to the Body and is for the Body. Furthermore, this verse...also shows that the one Body is determined by the one Spirit. Because there is one Spirit, there is one Body....We must keep the unique oneness of the Body because the Body and the Spirit are one.

The Spirit is the essence of the one Body. Without the Spirit, the Body is empty and has no life....Hence, the Body and the essence of the Body are one. It is impossible for the Body of Christ to have more than one essence. The unique essence of the Body is the Spirit.

Because there is one Spirit, there is only one Body. Moreover, there is only one circulation, one fellowship, of life in the Body. This circulation is the fellowship of the Body of Christ. All the local churches need to be in this unique fellowship. (*The Conclusion of the New Testament,* pp. 2178-2180, 2185-2186)

Further Reading: The Conclusion of the New Testament, msg. 203; *The Present Turmoil in the Lord's Recovery and the Direction of the Lord's Move Today,* ch. 1

Enlightenment and inspiration: _____

_____
_____
_____

Morning Nourishment

1 Cor. God is faithful, through whom you were called
1:9   into the fellowship of His Son, Jesus Christ our
       Lord.
10:16-17 The cup of blessing which we bless, is it not the fel-
       lowship of the blood of Christ? The bread which
       we break, is it not the fellowship of the body of
       Christ? Seeing that there is one bread, we who are
       many are one Body; for we all partake of the one
       bread.

The fellowship of the Body of Christ is expressed and practiced in our partaking of Christ's blood and body at the Lord's
table (1 Cor. 10:16, 21). As we partake of the table of the Lord,
we need to realize that this partaking is a fellowship, a participation, in the fellowship of the Lord's Body. We drink the cup
of the Lord and partake of the table of the Lord. The cup,
which is the cup of blessing, is a fellowship of the blood of
Christ, and the bread is a fellowship of the body of Christ.
Christ, the all-inclusive One, has given His body for us to eat
and His blood for us to drink that we may enjoy Him. As such
an all-inclusive One presenting Himself to us for our enjoyment, Christ is the embodiment of the processed Triune
God, who through death and resurrection, has become the
life-giving Spirit. Today the One who presents His body and
blood to us is Christ as the life-giving Spirit. As we enjoy Him
in partaking of His blood and body at His table, we express
and practice the fellowship of the Body of Christ, the unique
fellowship among the churches. (*The Conclusion of the New
Testament*, p. 2184)

Today's Reading

The fellowship among the churches is the fellowship of the
Body of Christ. In 1 Corinthians 10:16 and 17 Paul says, "The
cup of blessing which we bless, is it not the fellowship of the
blood of Christ? The bread which we break, is it not the

fellowship of the body of Christ? Seeing that there is one bread, we who are many are one Body; for we all partake of the one bread." The Greek word rendered "fellowship" here also means joint participation. In verse 16 fellowship refers to the believers' communion in the joint participation in the body and blood of Christ. This makes us, the participants of the Lord's blood and body, one not only with one another but also with the Lord. We, the participants, make ourselves identified with the Lord in the fellowship of His blood and body.

In verse 17 Paul speaks a strong word concerning the one bread and the one Body, saying that we are one bread, one Body, because we all partake of the one bread. Our joint partaking of the one bread makes us all one. This indicates that our partaking of Christ makes us all His one Body. The very Christ of whom we all partake constitutes us into His one Body.

If we isolate ourselves from the fellowship of the Body, we are not qualified to partake of the Lord's body, because the loaf on the table in the Lord's supper signifies the entire Body of Christ. To be sure, the loaf signifies the Lord's physical body sacrificed for us on the cross. This is one aspect of the significance of the bread. Another aspect of this significance is that the bread signifies the one Body. Hence, when we come together to partake of the Lord's table, we need to realize that the bread, the loaf, signifies all the churches. If the church in our locality or the churches in a particular region are isolated from the fellowship of the Body of Christ, we lose the ground and also the right to partake of this loaf. Whenever we come to the Lord's table, we come to practice the fellowship of the Body. The Lord's table is not simply a remembrance of the Lord; it is also a testimony that we who belong to Christ are one. (*The Conclusion of the New Testament,* pp. 2180-2181)

Further Reading: The Conclusion of the New Testament, msg. 203

Enlightenment and inspiration: _____

_____

_____

_____

Morning Nourishment

Acts 2:42	And they continued steadfastly in the teaching and the fellowship of the apostles, in the breaking of bread and the prayers.
1 Cor. 4:17	Because of this I have sent Timothy to you, who is my beloved and faithful child in the Lord, who will remind you of my ways which are in Christ, even as I teach everywhere in every church.

Among all the churches that compose the one universal Body of Christ, there is no organization, but there is the fellowship of the Body of Christ. This means that in the proper church life there is no organization, but there is much fellowship. Just as the human body does not have organization but does have circulation, so we should not have organization, but we should have fellowship. If all the churches stay in this circulation, in the fellowship of the Body, they will be healthy. However, the natural human thought is either to have organization or to have nothing to do with others. On the one hand, we should not have any organization among the churches; on the other hand, we should be open to have fellowship with all the churches. However, the church in a certain locality or the churches in a particular region may not be willing to have fellowship with other churches. This attitude is absolutely wrong. All the churches should remain in the fellowship of the Body. (*The Conclusion of the New Testament,* p. 2186)

Today's Reading

Teaching creates fellowship. If I were to teach foot-washing as a condition for receiving the saints, this teaching would immediately produce a particular fellowship. Fellowship comes from the teaching. There should be only one unique teaching—the teaching of the apostles. Furthermore, there should be one unique fellowship which is produced by the apostles' teaching. What we teach will produce a kind of fellowship. If we teach wrongly and differently from the apostles' teaching, our teaching will produce a sectarian, divisive fellowship....Wrong teaching produces wrong, divisive fellowship. We can have one way for one goal by keeping ourselves strictly in the limit of the apostles' teaching and the apostles' fellowship. There should not be another fellowship besides the apostles' fellowship.

In our work for the Lord, we must keep ourselves in the apostles' fellowship. If you have the burden to go to another locality to have the church life, you should do it with adequate fellowship from the church where you are. If you feel that you can raise up the church life in another city without fellowship with the brothers in the church in your locality, you will be raising up something outside the apostles' fellowship. The apostles' fellowship is universal in time and space. This fellowship includes all parts of the globe and includes all the centuries. Peter, Paul, and all the saints practicing the proper church life were in this fellowship. Anyone who would go out to another place to raise up the church life must have adequate fellowship with the church he has been meeting with. Otherwise, what he raises up will be something outside the apostles' fellowship and will cause division.

The principle of fellowship in the New Testament keeps us living the Body life....As members of the Body of Christ, we should not do things in a detached way....By keeping the principle of fellowship, we listen to one another. To listen to one another is to respect the Body. When the hand listens to the arm, the hand respects the body. To reject a member of the Body with whom you are connected, is to reject the Body itself. To disregard the Body and not listen to the Body is wrong. (*The God-ordained Way to Practice the New Testament Economy*, pp. 152-154)

Further Reading: The Conclusion of the New Testament, msgs. 203-204; The God-ordained Way to Practice the New Testament Economy, ch. 17; Life-study of Acts, msg. 12; The Triune God to Be Life to the Tripartite Man, chs. 16-19

Enlightenment and inspiration: _____

_____

_____

_____

Morning Nourishment

2 Cor.   The grace of the Lord Jesus Christ and the love of God
13:14   and the fellowship of the Holy Spirit be with you all.

1 John   That which we have seen and heard we report also
1:3   to you that you also may have fellowship with us,
and indeed our fellowship is with the Father and
with His Son Jesus Christ.

7   But if we walk in the light as He is in the light, we
have fellowship with one another, and the blood of
Jesus His Son cleanses us from every sin.

The fellowship of the Body of Christ is the fellowship of the
apostles—the divine fellowship between all the believers and the
Triune God. The term *the fellowship of the apostles* is used in Acts
2:42....Then, 1 John 1:3 tells us that the fellowship of the apostles
is not merely with us, the believers, but also with the Father and
the Son. Here John did not mention the Spirit directly, because he
was speaking in the Spirit. The Spirit was there already. The fellowship of the apostles is the fellowship of the Body of Christ, the
divine fellowship between all the believers and the Triune God.

The fellowship of the apostles is based upon the apostles'
teaching. Fellowship always comes after teaching. If there is no
teaching, there is no element or realm of the fellowship. Actually,
the teaching is the element and the realm of the fellowship. By
the Lord's mercy, today in the Lord's recovery we are under the
apostles' teaching and in the apostles' fellowship. The fellowship
of the recovery which we are in is the recovered fellowship of the
apostles....We need to see and have the boldness to say that we
are in the fellowship of the recovery which is the recovered apostles' fellowship. (*A Brief Presentation of the Lord's Recovery*,
pp. 38-39)

Today's Reading

The fellowship of the Body of Christ, which is the fellowship
among the churches, is the fellowship of the apostles. Acts 2:42
tells us that the believers continued steadfastly in the fellowship
of the apostles. Just as the teaching of the apostles is unique, so

the fellowship of the apostles also is unique. From this we see that all Christians should have one fellowship, the unique fellowship, which is the fellowship of the apostles.

This fellowship is mentioned in 1 John 1:3....The Greek word for fellowship is *koinonia* meaning joint participation, common participation. It is the issue of eternal life, and it is actually the flow of eternal life within all the believers who have received and possess the divine life. It is illustrated by the flow of the water of life in the New Jerusalem (Rev. 22:1). Hence, as indicated by Acts 2:42, all genuine believers are in this fellowship. It is carried on by the Spirit in our regenerated spirit. Therefore, it is called "the fellowship of the Holy Spirit" (2 Cor. 13:14) and "fellowship of [our] spirit" (Phil. 2:1). Such a fellowship was first the apostles' portion in enjoying the Father and Son through the Spirit. For this reason it is called the fellowship of the apostles in Acts 2:42 and "our [the apostles'] fellowship" in 1 John 1:3.

The word fellowship used in Acts 2:42 and 1 John 1:3 indicates the putting away of private interests and the joining with others for a certain common purpose. Hence, to have fellowship with the apostles, to be in the fellowship of the apostles, and to have fellowship with the Triune God in the apostles' fellowship, is to put away our private interests and join with the apostles and the Triune God for the carrying out of God's purpose. Our participation in the apostles' enjoyment of the Triune God is our joining with them and with the Triune God for His purpose, which is common to God, the apostles, and all the believers.

According to Acts 2:42, in the first church life there was only one fellowship, and that fellowship was of the apostles. The apostles' fellowship includes all genuine believers. In the church life in the Lord's recovery we follow and practice the fellowship of the apostles. (*The Conclusion of the New Testament*, pp. 2181-2182)

Further Reading: A Brief Presentation of the Lord's Recovery, "The Fellowship of the Churches in the Lord's Recovery"; *The Conclusion of the New Testament*, msgs. 203-204

Enlightenment and inspiration: _____

_____

_____

_____

Hymns, #737

1   Life eternal brings us
        Fellowship of life,
    Fellowship in Spirit,
        Saving us from strife.

2   Life eternal gives us
        Fellowship divine;
    Thus the Lord as Spirit
        May with us combine.

3   It is life in Spirit
        Brings this fellowship;
    Fellowship in Spirit
        Doth with grace equip.

4   We, by life's enabling,
        Fellowship aright;
    Fellowship in Spirit
        Brings us into light.

5   By the outward cleansing,
        Fellowship we keep;
    Inwardly anointed,
        Fellowship we reap.

6   Fellowship is deepened
        Thru the cross of death;
    Fellowship is lifted
        By the Spirit's breath.

7   Fellowship will free us
        From our sinful self;
    Fellowship will bring us
        Into God Himself.

Composition for prophecy with main point and sub-points: _____

The Unique Flow of the Divine Stream
for the Unique Blending of the Body of Christ

Scripture Reading: Gen. 2:10-14; Rev. 22:1; 1 Cor. 12:24;
16:10; Rom. 14:3; 15:7; 16:1-25

Day 1   I. **In the Scriptures the concept of the divine
stream, the unique flow, is crucial (Gen.
2:10-14; Psa. 46:4a; John 7:37-39; Rev. 22:1):**
A. The Bible reveals the flowing Triune God—the
Father as the fountain of life, the Son as the
spring of life, and the Spirit as the river of life
(Jer. 2:13; Psa. 36:9a; John 4:14; 7:37-39).
B. The source of the flow is the throne of God and of
the Lamb (Rev. 22:1).
C. In the Scriptures there is only one flow, only one
divine stream:
1. The divine stream, which has been flowing
throughout the generations, is uniquely one
(Gen. 2:10-14; Rev. 22:1).
2. Since there is only one divine stream and
since the flow is uniquely one, we need to
keep ourselves in this one flow.
D. Where the divine stream flows, we have the life
of God, the fellowship of the Body, the testimony
of Jesus, and the work of God.

Day 2   II. **The divine stream, the unique flow, is the
stream of the Lord's work (1 Cor. 16:10):**
A. There is a stream, which we may call the stream,
the current, of the work; where the stream flows,
there is the work of God.
B. The book of Acts reveals that in the move of
the Lord there is only one stream and that we
need to keep ourselves in this one stream
(cf. 15:35-41):
1. The flowing of the divine life, which started
on the day of Pentecost and has been flowing
throughout all generations to this day, is
just one stream.

2. The history of the church shows that throughout the generations there has been one stream of the Holy Spirit flowing all the time; many have been working for the Lord, but not all have been in the flowing of that one stream.

Day 3 III. **The divine stream, the unique flow, is a stream of fellowship (Acts 2:42; 1 John 1:3; 1 Cor. 10:16):**

A. The fellowship of the Body of Christ is the stream of the divine life; the divine fellowship is the reality of living in the Body of Christ (Rev. 22:1; 1 John 1:3).

B. What is needed today among the churches is more divine circulation, more fellowship (Act. 2:42; 2 Cor. 13:14).

Day 4 IV. **We need to imitate the apostle to bring the local churches into the fellowship of the Body of Christ (Rom. 14:3; 15:7-9, 25-33), and follow the apostle's footsteps to bring all the saints into the blending life of the entire Body of Christ (ch. 16):**

A. The last three chapters of Romans show us the blending and fellowship of the Body life brought forth through the apostle's receiving the believers according to God and Christ in order to demonstrate, show forth, and maintain the oneness of the Body of Christ (14:3; 15:7).

B. We need to follow the apostle's excellent pattern of bringing all the saints into the blending life of the entire Body of Christ through his recommendations and greetings, which show both the mutual concern among the saints and the mutual fellowship among the churches (16:1-16, 20-25).

C. Among us we should have the blending of all the individual members of the Body of Christ, the blending of all the churches in certain districts, the blending of all the co-workers, and the blending of all the elders (1 Cor. 12:24).

Day 5

D. We must have the reality of the fellowship and blending of the Body of Christ; otherwise, regardless of how much we pursue and how simple and humble we are, sooner or later there will be problems, even divisions, among us:

1. The unique relationship, fellowship, and blending of all the local churches should be as much as practicality allows, without boundaries of states, provinces, or nations.

2. The clustering and moving together of neighboring churches should be as much as possible, without the abolishing of the local administrations in business affairs.

3. All the local churches on the entire globe should be absolutely one by being in the oneness of the Spirit and in the one accord of our spirit, soul, and mind (Eph. 4:3-4a; Acts 1:14; Phil. 1:27).

4. All the local churches should be absolutely one in the realm of five crucial things:

   a. The growth of life for the testimony of Jesus Christ.

   b. The preaching of the gospel.

   c. The spreading of the Lord's recovery.

   d. The building up of the Body of Christ.

   e. The accomplishment of God's eternal economy.

Day 6

V. **For the Lord's move in His recovery both locally and universally, we all need to be Body-conscious in one accord and Body-centered in oneness:**

A. "In our consideration the Body should be first and the local churches should be second....All the local churches are and should be one Body universally, doctrinally and practically. Otherwise, where is the unique church of God and the unique one new man for the fulfilling of God's economy!" (*One Body and One Spirit,* p. 24).

B. Not one local church is the Body; every local

church is a part of the Body; there are many
local churches but there are never many bodies
(Eph. 4:4a).

C. "The purpose of the blending is to usher us all
into the reality of the Body of Christ. I treasure
the local churches, as you do. But I treasure the
local churches because of a purpose. The local
churches are the procedure to bring me into the
Body of Christ. The churches are the Body, but
the churches may not have the reality of the
Body of Christ. Thus, we need to be in the local
churches so that we can be ushered, or brought,
into the reality of the Body of Christ" (*The Practical Points concerning Blending,* p. 10).

Morning Nourishment

John
4:14 But whoever drinks of the water that I will give him shall by no means thirst forever; but the water that I will give him will become in him a fountain of water springing up into eternal life.

7:38-39 He who believes into Me, as the Scripture said, out of his innermost being shall flow rivers of living water. But this He said concerning the Spirit...

Acts
2:33 Therefore having been exalted to the right hand of God and having received the promise of the Holy Spirit from the Father, He has poured out this which you both see and hear.

How many times throughout the Scriptures God is spoken of as a flowing stream of water! "You cause them to drink of the river of Your pleasures. / For with You is the fountain of life..." (Psa. 36:8-9). The Lord Jesus tells us that the water that He gives will become a fountain of living water springing up unto eternal life (John 4:14). He says again that whoever is thirsty may come to Him and drink, and whoever believes into Him will have rivers of living water flowing from within him (John 7:37-38). All these words relate to one thing—that God has flowed out and is still flowing on this earth into humanity as the life. We may ask, In what form has God flowed out? He has flowed out first in His Son, in Christ; and then He has flowed out as the Spirit. God is the fountain, the very source; Christ the Son is the spring, the reservoir, of this divine water; and the Holy Spirit is the living stream, flowing all the time. (*The Divine Stream*, pp. 9-10)

Today's Reading

On the day of Pentecost the Lord poured Himself out in the Holy Spirit. Notice the word "poured" in Acts 2:33. He poured out the Holy Spirit, and the Holy Spirit became the flowing stream of the divine water. For almost two thousand years since that time, the Holy Spirit has been flowing in this world. This flowing has never stopped and will flow to eternity. God the Father is the very source. Christ the Son is the reservoir, the Rock smitten that the divine water stored within may be released....This living water...is the very Spirit of the life of God. The Holy Spirit is the flowing Spirit of the divine life....He has poured out the Holy Spirit, flowing with the divine life. From that time there is a flowing of the divine life, and this flowing is the Holy Spirit Himself.

The flowing of the divine life, which started on the day of Pentecost and has been flowing throughout all generations to this very day, is just one stream. Wherever it goes, wherever it flows, it is not many streams; it is only one....It was one in Jerusalem, one to Antioch, one to Asia, one to Europe, and one everywhere it has flowed. Please be clear that there have never been two streams. There is only one stream, and you have to keep yourself in this one stream.

If you read the Acts and the Epistles written by the apostle Paul, you will see that quite a number of people at that time who were preaching the gospel and working for the Lord were not in the stream....In the first chapter of Philippians the apostle tells us that there were some who preached the gospel because of envy....Although they preached the gospel, they were not in the one stream of the Holy Spirit. In the book of Acts you can find another example....Barnabas was working with the apostle Paul. Both were in the one stream. But after a certain time, Barnabas for some reason would not agree to go along with the apostle Paul. The two were divided. Do you find any record in the Acts of Barnabas after that division? No! He was out of the stream. He was still working for the Lord, but he was out of the stream....If you study carefully the history of the church, you will find that throughout the generations there has been one stream of the Holy Spirit flowing all the time. Many have been working for the Lord, but not all have been in the flowing of that one stream. If you will accept the mercy and the grace of the Lord, you will be brought into that very stream that is flowing today. (*The Divine Stream*, pp. 10, 12-13)

Further Reading: The Divine Stream

Enlightenment and inspiration: _____

_____

_____

_____

Morning Nourishment

Psa. For with You is the fountain of life; in Your light we
36:9 see light.

46:4 There is a river whose streams gladden the city of
God...

Rev. And he showed me a river of water of life, bright as
22:1 crystal, proceeding out of the throne of God and of
the Lamb...

1 Cor. Now if Timothy comes, see that he is with you
16:10 without fear; for he is working the work of the
Lord, even as I am.

This stream is also the stream of God's work. Where the stream flows, there is the work of God. This is clear in the book of Acts, a book which speaks to us of the work of God. What is that kind of work which is the work of God? It is a work in the stream of living water. Where the stream of living water flows, there is the work of God. God works along the flowing of the stream of the divine life. If you consider the whole record of the book of Acts, you will see the picture quite clearly. On the day of Pentecost this stream of divine life flowed out of God Himself in Christ with ruling power from the throne. It began to flow from Jerusalem. From there it flowed to Antioch, and then from Antioch it turned to the West; it flowed to Asia, and through Asia it flowed to Macedonia, to Europe. Here is a picture of the flowing of the stream of divine life, and with the flowing of this stream is the work of God. By flowing God works; by flowing God preaches His gospel; by flowing God brings people to be saved. There is a stream which we could call the stream or the current of the work. Where it flows, there is the work of God. (*The Divine Stream*, pp. 6-7)

Today's Reading

Notice that there is no end, no conclusion, to the book of Acts....The twenty-eight chapters in our Bible are just the record of sixty or seventy years of history. There is an opening, but no closing, no conclusion. This is because this stream of life is still flowing and never stops flowing. The history of the church shows

that this stream has continued to flow from generation to generation right up to this very day, and it is flowing still. Where it flows,
there is the life of God; where it flows, there is the fellowship of the
Body; where it flows, there is the testimony of Jesus; and where it
flows, there is also the work of God. It is the stream of life, the
stream of fellowship, the stream of testimony, and the stream of
the work of God.

Brothers and sisters, we must be in this stream. If we are not
in this stream, we are out of life, we are out of the fellowship of the
Body, we are out of the testimony of the Lord Jesus, and we are
out of the work of God. Oh, if we are simply in this stream, we will
have everything....God is in the Lamb, and the Lamb is on the
throne, and this stream flows out of this throne. If you have this
stream, you have the throne, you have the Lamb and you have
God within the Lamb. If you have this stream you have everything. If you are in this stream, then you are in God, you are in the
Lamb with the throne, you are in the life, you are in the fellowship, you are in the testimony, and you are in the work of God. Are
you in the stream? You need to know. If you are not in the stream,
you will have to make a turn; you will have to have a crisis. We
must be in the stream!

In the universe there is a divine stream....We can trace this
stream from the beginning of the Bible right to the end....It is still
flowing today. It is flowing, flowing all the time, and will be flowing to eternity....It can never and will never cease.

This stream has flowed back to the Western world as a supply
to His Body. We look to the Lord that it will be increasing in this
country and even to all parts of the world. May we remember this
in our prayers, and may we be ready to go along with the Lord
that this stream may have a free way to flow without any hin-
drance in us. We must be faithful to the flowing of this stream of
the divine life, of the fellowship of the Body, of the testimony of the
Lord Jesus, and of the work of God. (*The Divine Stream,* pp. 7-8)

Further Reading: The Divine Stream

Enlightenment and inspiration: _____

_____
_____
_____

Morning Nourishment

Acts 2:42	And they continued steadfastly in the teaching and the fellowship of the apostles...
1 John 1:3	That which we have seen and heard we report also to you that you also may have fellowship with us, and indeed our fellowship is with the Father and with His Son Jesus Christ.
1 Cor. 10:16	The cup of blessing which we bless, is it not the fellowship of the blood of Christ? The bread which we break, is it not the fellowship of the body of Christ?
2 Cor. 13:14	The grace of the Lord Jesus Christ and the love of God and the fellowship of the Holy Spirit be with you all.

From this picture of the stream in the Scriptures, we may realize that it is also a stream of fellowship. Consider the situation of the New Jerusalem. In the whole city there is only one street, and in the midst of that street is the stream of living water. By contemplating this scene we realize that this stream is the stream of fellowship. It flows throughout the entire city, and the whole city can only have fellowship through or by this stream of living water. This reveals that the fellowship of the Body of Christ is the stream of divine life....As the stream of the divine life flows within us, there is the fellowship of the Body among us. This fellowship started from the day of Pentecost, and from Jerusalem it flowed to Antioch, to Asia, to Europe, and then to America and throughout the world. The fellowship of the Body which we are enjoying is such a tremendous thing. We are in this stream of the fellowship of the Body, and this flowing is ever increasing and being enriched. The more it flows, the greater and the richer it becomes. (*The Divine Stream*, p. 5)

Today's Reading

The flowing of this stream of the Holy Spirit is the fellowship of the Body of Christ. It is similar to the circulation of the blood in our physical bodies. The blood is flowing all the time from one part to another and then back again. In just such a way is the stream of the Holy Spirit as the fellowship of the Body flowing among the saints upon this earth.

When I was young, Brother Nee came one day to have a talk with me. I was a young learner under his hand, and many times he gave me some basic lessons. He said, "Brother, do you know that we can never go to any place to start a work unless the current of the Holy Spirit is there already?" Oh, how I have remembered this word! Unless the current of the Holy Spirit is already in a place, you and I can never go there to work. Brother Nee continued to say: "Oh, brother, if you realize where the current of the Holy Spirit is, simply go along with it! To work there for the Lord will be a rest to you; it will be a bed upon which you can lie. The work in the flowing of the Holy Spirit is not a burden, but a rest." I cannot tell you how much these words have helped me. From that time I have learned the lesson that I must go along with the flowing of the stream of the Holy Spirit. I cannot go to any place to work for the Lord or to start a work for the Lord without the flowing of the current of the Holy Spirit. I am unable to do that, I am not qualified to do that, and I am not ordered by the Lord to do that. What I must do is just go along with the flowing.

Let me give you a further personal word. I had no intention of coming to the United States, but the flowing of the Holy Spirit carried me here. I could not help it. Furthermore, my intention was that I would soon return to the Far East. But the flowing is still westward, and I could not return. My direction was eastward, but the flowing of the Spirit was westward. All I can do is simply be carried along by this flow. How wonderful to be in this stream! Oh, here is the life, here is the fellowship, here is the testimony, and here is the work of God!

What we must do today is just go along with the stream, just subject ourselves to the current of the work of the Holy Spirit. In this matter I have no personal liberty. It is not according to my thoughts, but according to His flowing. (*The Divine Stream,* pp. 14-16)

Further Reading: The Divine Stream

Enlightenment and inspiration: _____

_____

_____

_____

Morning Nourishment

1 Cor. 12:24	...But God has blended the body together, giving more abundant honor to the *member* that lacked.
Rom. 15:7	Therefore receive one another, as Christ also received you to the glory of God.
16:3-4	Greet Prisca and Aquila, my fellow workers in Christ Jesus, who risked their own necks for my life, to whom not only I give thanks, but also all the churches of the Gentiles.
20	Now the God of peace will crush Satan under your feet shortly. The grace of our Lord Jesus be with you.

Fellowship tempers us; fellowship adjusts us; fellowship harmonizes us; and fellowship mingles us. We should forget about whether we are slow or quick and just fellowship with others. We should not do anything without fellowshipping with the other saints who are coordinating with us. Fellowship requires us to stop when we are about to do something. In our coordination in the church life, in the Lord's work, we all have to learn not to do anything without fellowship.

Among us we should have the blending of all the individual members of the Body of Christ, the blending of all the churches in certain districts, the blending of all the co-workers, and the blending of all the elders. Blending means that we should always stop to fellowship with others. Then we will receive many benefits. If we isolate and seclude ourselves, we will lose much spiritual profit. Learn to fellowship. Learn to be blended. From now on, the churches should come together frequently to be blended. We may not be used to it, but after we begin to practice blending a few times, we will acquire the taste for it. This is the most helpful thing in the keeping of the oneness of the universal Body of Christ. (*The Divine and Mystical Realm,* p. 87)

Today's Reading

The last three chapters of Romans show us the blending and fellowship of the Body life brought forth through the apostle's receiving according to God and Christ....Romans 16 gives us an excellent pattern of the apostle in bringing all the saints into the blending life of the entire Body of Christ. It is in such a life that we can truly reign in life.

We must follow in the footsteps of the apostle. He brought us into the blending life of the entire Body of Christ by recommendations and greetings that the God of peace may crush Satan under our feet and that we may enjoy the rich grace of Christ (vv. 1-16, 21-24, 20). In Romans 16 the apostle Paul greeted the saints, one by one, mentioning at least twenty-seven names.... Moreover, he greeted the saints generally. This shows us that he had a considerable amount of knowledge, understanding, and care with regard to every one of them. Such recommendations and greetings show both the mutual concern among the saints and the mutual fellowship among the churches. It is by the churches' fellowship in the Body that the God of peace will crush Satan under our feet and we will be able to enjoy the rich grace of Christ. This grace is the manifestation of the Triune God in His embodiment in three aspects—the Father, the Son, and the Spirit.

We must have the reality of the fellowship and blending of the Body of Christ. Otherwise, regardless of how much we pursue and how simple and humble we are, sooner or later there will be problems, even divisions, among us. Hence, we must be governed by the vision of the Body and follow in the footsteps of the apostle by bringing all the saints in all the churches into the blending life of the entire Body of Christ. This is to reign in life, and by such reigning we give glory to God. This glory is the New Jerusalem, the universal incorporation of the union and mingling of divinity with humanity, in which God will be completely glorified and His economy will be fully accomplished. (*The Experience of God's Organic Salvation Equaling Reigning in Christ's Life,* pp. 70-71)

Further Reading: The Divine and Mystical Realm, ch. 6; *The Experience of God's Organic Salvation Equaling Reigning in Christ's Life,* msg. 6

Enlightenment and inspiration: _____

_____

_____

_____

Morning Nourishment

Eph. 4:3-4 Being diligent to keep the oneness of the Spirit in the uniting bond of peace: One Body and one Spirit...

Acts 1:14 These all continued steadfastly with one accord in prayer...

Phil. 1:27 Only, conduct yourselves in a manner worthy of the gospel of Christ...that you stand firm in one spirit, with one soul striving together *along* with the faith of the gospel.

All the local churches on the entire globe should be absolutely one by being in the oneness of the Spirit and in the one accord of our spirit, soul, and mind.

All the local churches should be absolutely one in the realm of five crucial things: (1) the growth of life for the testimony of Jesus Christ; (2) the preaching of the gospel; (3) the spreading of the Lord's recovery; (4) the building up of the Body of Christ; and (5) the accomplishment of God's eternal economy. We should be one in all these things.

We do not need to be one in certain things concerning the administration of the church. Whether the church in a certain locality should buy a piece of land in order to build a hall or not is a local affair. But in the growth of life for the testimony of the Lord, in the preaching of the gospel, in the spreading of the Lord's recovery, in the building up of the Body of Christ, and in the accomplishment of God's eternal economy, we have to be one universally. (*One Body and One Spirit*, p. 23)

Today's Reading

The unique relationship, fellowship, and blending of all the local churches should be as much as practicality allows, without boundaries of states, provinces, or nations. If we are divided by any kind of boundary, the church becomes no longer a Body; rather, it becomes a corpse. A divided body is a corpse. We have been unaware of the fact that in the past five years the testimony of the recovery has been very much weakened. This is why we have lost our impact. In nearly every locality the number is too small with a low rate of increase. We all love the Lord, and we are in the recovery. We all keep the truth and teach the truth. Nevertheless, there is very little increase among us.

We need to reconsider our way (Hag. 1:5, 7). We are rich in truth, and we are pure in following the Lord, yet our increase is too low. Nearly everywhere it is the same. Based on this one fact of the low rate of increase among us, we should all humble ourselves before the Lord. The rate of increase measures where we are.

Are the churches in every area willing to be blended together as one? There may be fifteen churches in a particular region, but the question is whether or not they would be willing to be blended together. We may like to be independent under the cloak of being local....The Bible reveals to us that all the saints and all the local churches are one Body.

All the local churches on the globe today should be one. Today, unlike in Paul's time, travel and communication to nearly anywhere on the earth are very convenient. Because of this, the churches today should be blended much more than they were in Paul's time. Not only according to the revelation of the Bible but also according to the modern conveniences, we should be one, and we should be blended together as much as practicality allows.

The clustering and the moving together of neighboring churches should be as much as possible....Our blending together should not be in name only; we must take some action. The local administration still exists, but in the spiritual element all the churches should be blended together as one....We have to learn to be blended with other churches. There may be only fifteen saints in a certain locality, and they can have a group meeting there. They even have the freedom to declare that they are the church in that locality, but they must also learn to be blended together with the neighboring churches. When we are blended together as one church, we will have the impact. (*One Body and One Spirit*, pp. 19-21)

Further Reading: One Body and One Spirit, ch. 1

Enlightenment and inspiration: _____

_____

_____

_____

Morning Nourishment

Eph. And He subjected all things under His feet and gave
1:22-23 Him *to be* Head over all things to the church, which
is His Body...

4:4-6 One Body and one Spirit, even as also you were
called in one hope of your calling; one Lord, one
faith, one baptism; one God and Father of all, who is
over all and through all and in all.

For the Lord's move in His recovery both locally and universally, we all need to be Body-conscious in one accord and Body-
centered in oneness. In one accord we should be Body-conscious.
In oneness we should be Body-centered. In our consideration the
Body should be first and the local churches should be second....What a shame it is for any local church to declare its auton-
omy! To teach that the local churches are absolutely autonomous
is to divide the Body of Christ. All the local churches are and
should be one Body universally, doctrinally, and practically. Otherwise, where is the unique church of God and the unique one
new man for the fulfilling of God's economy?! (*One Body and One
Spirit*, p. 24)

Today's Reading

We may think that the local churches are the goal of God's
economy. However, they are not the goal, but the procedure God
takes to reach the goal of His economy. We should not forget that
the local churches are not God's goal....Since the time of Brother
Nee the local churches have become a very precious item in our
Christian life. Some of the saints may be disappointed when they
hear that the local churches are not God's goal. Nevertheless, if
we are just in the local churches and do not go on, we are far off
from God's goal.

According to Ephesians 1:22-23, the goal of God's economy is the
church, which is Christ's Body. Some may say that since the church
is the Body of Christ and since we are in the church, we should also
be in the Body. They are right doctrinally, but not practically....We
have the term *the Body of Christ* and we have the doctrine of the

Body of Christ, but where is the practicality and reality of the Body of Christ? Have you ever touched the practicality of the Body of Christ? Have you ever been in the reality of the Body of Christ?

We all need to consider this matter. We have the term and we have the doctrine, but practically, we do not have the reality. The purpose of the blending is to usher us all into the reality of the Body of Christ. I treasure the local churches, as you do. But I treasure the local churches because of a purpose. The local churches are the procedure to bring me into the Body of Christ. The churches are the Body, but the churches may not have the reality of the Body of Christ. Thus, we need to be in the local churches so that we can be ushered, or brought, into the reality of the Body of Christ.

Not only so, eventually, the book of Revelation does have a consummation. In this consummation all the seven lampstands disappear. In the first chapter we see the seven lampstands. But in the last two chapters we see only one city. Eventually, the local churches will be over. Only the Body will remain and remain forever, and this Body of Christ is the unique tabernacle as God's dwelling place on this earth, the unique bride of the Lamb (Rev. 21:2-3).

Therefore, we must pay much more attention to the Body of Christ than to the local churches. This does not mean that I annul the teaching of the local churches. We still need it. As a person we have a physical frame. That is our body. But a body by itself is a carcass. A physical body needs an inner life. Today the church is the same. On the one hand, it does have a frame, a body, but this frame is not the nature, the essence, or the element of the church. Ephesians 4 tells us the church is the Body, and within this church is the Spirit, the Lord, and the Father (vv. 4-6). The Father is the source, the Lord is the element, and the Spirit is the essence of the Body. These four entities are built together. (*The Practical Points concerning Blending,* pp. 9-10, 23-24)

Further Reading: One Body and One Spirit, ch. 1; The Practical Points concerning Blending, chs. 1, 3-4; Elders' Training, Book 4: Other Crucial Matters concerning the Practice of the Lord's Recovery, ch. 4

Enlightenment and inspiration: _____
_____
_____
_____

Hymns, #909

1   In the stream! in the stream! let us work
        for the Lord,
    By His mind, in His way, as revealed in
        His Word;
    In the flow of His life let us work with His
        pow'r
    For His Kingdom and Church in the time
        of His hour.

        In the stream! in the stream!
        Let us work in the stream!
        In the stream! in the stream!
        We'll work as in the heav'nly team!

2   In the stream! in the stream! let us work
        with the Lord
    In the flow of the Spirit, as taught by
        His Word;
    Never working by self, independent and
        free,
    But in service related in full harmony.

3   In the stream! in the stream! let us work
        in the Lord,
    With the Church, with the saints, in the
        light of His Word;
    Give the Word, life supply to the people
        in need,
    Thus fulfilling God's plan, in His flow
        we'll proceed.

Composition for prophecy with main point and sub-points: _____

_____

_____

_____

_____

_____

_____

_____

_____

_____

_____

_____

_____

_____

_____

_____

_____

_____

_____

_____

_____

_____

_____

_____

_____

_____

_____

_____

_____

_____

_____

_____

_____

_____

_____

God's Unique Work

Scripture Reading: 1 Cor. 3:6-9, 12; 15:58; 16:10; Eph. 4:11-12

Day 1   I. **God's economy is centered on one thing—God's unique work (1 Cor. 15:58; 16:10):**
  A. Throughout the ages God has only one work, and that is to work Himself into man; God's unique work in the universe and throughout all the ages and generations is to work Himself in Christ into His chosen people, making Himself one with them (Gal. 1:15-16a; 2:20; 4:19; Eph. 3:16-17a).

Day 2   B. If we realize that God desires to work Himself into His chosen people and if we realize that this is all that we need, then the goal of our work will be to minister Christ to others so that the Triune God may build Himself into their inner being (1 Cor. 3:6-9).
  C. Our work in the recovery today is to minister God into people; we need to practice one thing—to minister the processed Triune God into others so that He may build Himself into their inner man (v. 12).
  D. The one unique work of the ministry is to carry out God's economy to work Himself into man for the building up of the Body of Christ, consummating in the New Jerusalem (Eph. 3:9-11; 4:11-12; Rev. 21:2).

  II. **All the co-workers should do the same one work universally for the unique Body; the starting point of the work is the oneness of the Body:**
  A. The Lord's recovery is to recover the oneness of the Body; this means that in the recovery we must see the universal Body and do everything in the limitation, the regulation, of the one Body (Rom. 12:5; 1 Cor. 12:12).

B. The work in the Lord's recovery is for the building up of the local churches unto the building up of the universal Body of Christ (Eph. 2:21-22).

Day 3

C. "The church, which is His Body," includes the churches, the ministry, and the work (1:22b-23a):

1. The churches are the Body expressed locally, the ministry is the Body in function, and the work is the Body seeking increase.

2. The church is the life of the Body in miniature; the ministry is the function of the Body in service; the work is the reaching out of the Body in growth.

D. The basic principle of the churches, the ministry, and the work is the Body:

1. All three are from the Body, in the Body, and for the Body.

2. All three are different manifestations of the one Body, so they are all interdependent and interrelated.

3. The Body is the governing law of the life and work of the children of God today.

Day 4
&
Day 5

III. **The co-workers need to carry out a threefold work to build up the Body of Christ—the work in the stage of incarnation, the work in the stage of inclusion, and the work in the stage of intensification:**

A. All the co-workers must see the three stages, the three sections, of Christ: incarnation—the stage of Christ in the flesh; inclusion—the stage of Christ as the life-giving Spirit; and intensification—the stage of Christ as the sevenfold intensified life-giving Spirit (John 1:14; 1 Cor. 15:45b; Rev. 1:4; 3:1; 4:5; 5:6).

B. We need to know Christ and to experience, enjoy, and gain Him according to all that He has accomplished and is accomplishing in the three stages of His full ministry (Phil. 3:8-10a).

C. We emphasize these three words—*incarnation, inclusion,* and *intensification*—and stress the facts that incarnation produces redeemed people, that inclusion produces the churches, and that intensification produces the overcomers to build up the Body, which consummates in the New Jerusalem as the unique goal of God's economy.

Day 6

D. If we are carrying out a threefold work according to the stages of Christ's history and full ministry, we will work not only to produce redeemed ones and work to establish churches but will also work to build up the Body consummating in the New Jerusalem:

1. The foundation is the work in the stage of incarnation, the building up is the work in the stage of inclusion, and the completion of the building is the work in the stage of intensification.

2. "I would urge you to consider this matter of intensification and to pray desperately, saying, 'Lord, I must advance. I need Your grace to bring me onward. I do not want to remain in the work of incarnation nor even in the work of inclusion. I want to advance from inclusion to intensification. Lord, You have been intensified sevenfold, and I pray that I also will be intensified sevenfold to overcome the degradation of the church that the Body may be built up to consummate the New Jerusalem'" (*Incarnation, Inclusion, and Intensification,* p. 22).

IV. **Today there are four kinds of workers:**

A. The first are the co-workers who match the need of the ministry of God in the present age; this is a small group of people who have been dealt with by the Lord and who are in one accord.

B. The second kind are the younger co-workers; they are willing to receive the direction and to come under the coordination of the older co-workers, and they are willing to follow and to learn in humility.

C. The third kind are those who are unwilling to submit to the senior co-workers, who do not belong to the denominations, yet who are happy to remain in fellowship with us.

D. The fourth kind are the preachers and free evangelists among the denominations.

E. What we need today are the first and second kind of co-workers.

F. Concerning the third and fourth kind of co-workers, we can only let them choose their own pathway; with some people God has not assigned them to take the same way as we do, and we dare not say anything to them.

G. Whatever the situation may be, we are here to do the work that God has committed to us; we cannot interfere with others' work, and we are not here tearing down others' work.

Morning Nourishment

Eph. And to enlighten all *that they may see* what the econ-
3:9 omy of the mystery is, which throughout the ages has
been hidden in God, who created all things.
16-17 That He would grant you, according to the riches of
His glory, to be strengthened with power through His
Spirit into the inner man, that Christ may make
His home in your hearts through faith...
2 Cor. Therefore we do not lose heart; but though our
4:16 outer man is decaying, yet our inner *man* is being
renewed day by day.

Throughout the ages, God has only one work, and that is to work Himself into man....Why did God create the universe? Why did He create man?...What is God trying to accomplish? This is an important question. If God wants to do something, and you do not know about it, your Christian life is meaningless. You may think that God's intention is for you to have joy and peace. It is true that God wants you to have joy and peace, but these things are not God's center. God is not merely giving you peace, blessings, forgiveness, eternal life, and so forth; His central thought is to work Himself into man. What is the ultimate goal of God in the old creation as well as in the new? It is to work Himself into man. This is God's goal. God's redemption is for this goal. He created the universe in order to put man in it, and the purpose for Him to have man is to work Himself into him....This is His desire; He wants to work Himself into man.

We have to remember all the time that the need today is for God to work Himself into us, rather than for us to work for God. All those who will only work for God without allowing God to work in them will eventually be rejected. Only those who allow God to work in them through various circumstances, people, matters, and events will be blessed by Him. (*Messages Given during the Resumption of Watchman Nee's Ministry*, pp. 107, 111)

Today's Reading

The problem today is that no one is willing to contain God. Our eyes need to be opened. If there is such a group of people, God will have a way here in this place, and man will receive the blessing. God has no intention for you to love your wife or to hate your wife. God has no intention for the wife to submit to the husband or to rebel against the husband. God has only one intention, and that is to work Himself into man.

Some have asked me if they can quit their job to serve the Lord full-time. I told them bluntly that it does not mean anything for them to remain in their jobs, and it does not mean anything for them to quit their jobs and be a preacher. The question is not whether or not one should be a preacher, but whether or not one will allow the Lord to work in him. God's work in the old creation is outside of man. His work in the new creation is within man. One day, the work of the old creation will pass away. But the work of the new creation will remain until the New Jerusalem; it will never pass away but will have eternal value.

For a man to do good apart from God is as worthless as it is for him to commit sin apart from God. Of course, within the span of time, all virtues are better than evil. But in eternity, both are worthless. Time is in God's hand, and God puts the man He gained into this "furnace" with the purpose of working Himself into man, so that man can be in God and God can be in man.... God's intention today is to fill our inclinations and our character with God's nature and character. In the end, God will become our content, and His fullness will be mingled with us....His purpose is for man to be like Him. He has no intention to merely improve us a little. This is man's natural concept. The human ethical mind thinks that all a person needs to do is to change the wrongs and make them right. But God's thought is not concerning good and evil, but concerning His working Himself into us. (*Messages Given during the Resumption of Watchman Nee's Ministry,* pp. 109-110, 126-127)

Further Reading: Messages Given during the Resumption of Watchman Nee's Ministry, chs. 20-24, 26

Enlightenment and inspiration: _____

_____

_____

_____

Morning Nourishment

Gal. But when it pleased God, who set me apart from my
1:15-16 mother's womb and called me through His grace, to
reveal His Son in me...
2:20 I am crucified with Christ; and *it is* no longer I *who*
live, but *it is* Christ *who* lives in me; and the *life* which
I now live in the flesh I live in faith...
4:19 My children, with whom I travail again in birth until
Christ is formed in you.
1 Cor. Therefore, my beloved brothers, be steadfast, immov-
15:58 able, always abounding in the work of the Lord,
knowing that your labor is not in vain in the Lord.

God's economy is centered on one thing—God's unique work.
God's unique work in the universe and throughout all the ages
and generations is to work Himself in Christ into His chosen people, making Himself one with them. This involves the mingling of
divinity with humanity.

In order to work Himself into us, God became a man and lived
a human life on earth. Then He passed through death and entered into resurrection and ascension, becoming the consummated life-giving Spirit ready to come into us. When He came into
us, He regenerated our spirit. Now He is working in us to increase
Himself in us and to build Himself into us. (*Life-study of 1 &
2 Samuel*, pp. 195-196)

Today's Reading

A person may be according to the heart of God and yet be without
God, not having God wrought into him. The fall of David illustrates
the fact that even if we are a person according to God, if we do not
have God wrought into us, we are no better than others. What is the
value of being according to the heart of God if we do not have God
wrought into our hearts? If we realize that God desires to work
Himself into His chosen people and if we realize that this is what
we all need, then the goal of our work will be to minister Christ to
others so that the Triune God may build Himself into their being.

Our work in the recovery today is to minister God to people.

Yes, we need to save sinners and to feed the saints and perfect them. The crucial matter, however, is that we minister God to others. The God whom we minister is not just the building God— He is also the builded God. If we fail to minister God in this way, our work will be wood, grass, and stubble (1 Cor. 3:12).

I would ask you to reconsider the work you are doing for the Lord. Perhaps you have opened up a region or have brought many people to God. But I ask you this question: How much of Christ as the embodiment of the Triune God has been wrought into those whom you have brought to God? If we are sincere and genuine, we will humble ourselves and confess that not very much of the Triune God has been wrought into the ones we have brought to God. Therefore, we need to practice one thing—to minister the processed Triune God into others so that He may build Himself into their inner man. In every aspect of our work—preaching the gospel, feeding the believers, perfecting the saints—the intrinsic element must be that we minister the building and builded God to others. I would urge you to pray that the Lord would teach you to work in this way.

The processed Triune God is embodied in Christ and realized as the consummated Spirit. This is the God whom we worship, preach, and minister to others. Today He is building Himself into His redeemed people in order to produce a house with Himself as the element and also with something from their redeemed and uplifted humanity. This house is the church, the Body of Christ. This house is the enlargement, the expansion, of Christ, the embodiment of the Triune God realized as the Spirit. As we carry out the God-ordained way in the four steps of begetting, nourishing, perfecting, and building, our work must be based upon the processed Triune God, who is building Himself into His chosen people. (*Life-study of 1 & 2 Samuel,* pp. 200-201)

Further Reading: Life-study of 1 & 2 Samuel, msg. 30; *The Ministry of the New Testament and the Teaching and Fellowship of the Apostles,* ch. 1; *Further Consideration of the Eldership, the Region of the Work, and the Care for the Body of Christ,* ch. 1

Enlightenment and inspiration: _____

_____

_____

_____

Morning Nourishment

Eph. And He...gave Him *to be* Head over all things to the
1:22-23 church, which is His Body...
4:11-12 And He Himself gave some as apostles and some
as prophets and some as evangelists and some as
shepherds and teachers, for the perfecting of the
saints unto the work of the ministry, unto the building up of the Body of Christ.

The ministry, the work, and the churches are quite different in
function and sphere, but they are really coordinated and interrelated. Ephesians 4 speaks of the Body of Christ, but no discrimi-
nation is made there between the churches, the work, and the
ministry. The saints of the churches, the apostles of the work, and
the different ministers of the ministry are all considered in the
light of, and in relation to, the Body of Christ. Because whether it
be the local church, the ministry, or the work, all are in the church.
They are really one; so while it is necessary to distinguish between them in order to understand them better, we cannot really
separate them. Those who are in the different spheres of the
church need to see the reality of the Body of Christ and act
relatedly as a body. They should not, because of difference of re-
sponsibilities, settle themselves into watertight compartments.
(*The Normal Christian Church Life,* pp. 186-187)

Today's Reading

"The church, which is His Body," includes the churches, the
ministry, and the work. The churches are the Body expressed locally, the ministry is the Body in function, and the work is the
Body seeking increase. All three are different manifestations of
the one Body, so they are all interdependent and interrelated.
None can move, or even exist, by itself. In fact, their relationship is
so intimate and vital that none can be right itself without being
rightly adjusted to the others. The church cannot go on without
receiving the help of the ministry and without giving help to the
work; the work cannot exist without the sympathy of the ministry
and the backing of the church; and the ministry can only function

when there is the church and the work.

This is most important. In the previous chapters we have sought to show their respective functions and spheres; now the danger is lest, failing to understand the spiritual nature of the things of God, we should not only try to *distinguish* between them, but *sever* them into separate units, thus losing the interrelatedness of the Body. However clear the distinction between them, we must remember that they are all in the church. Consequently, they must move and act as one, for no matter what their specific functions and spheres, they are all in one Body.

So on the one hand, we differentiate between them in order to understand them, and on the other hand, we bear in mind that they are all related as a body. It is not that a few gifted men, recognizing their own ability, take it upon themselves to minister with the gifts they possess; nor that a few persons, conscious of call, form themselves into a working association; nor is it that a number of like-minded believers unite and call themselves a church. All must be on the ground of the Body. The church is the life of the Body in miniature; the ministry is the functioning of the Body in service; the work is the reaching out of the Body in growth. Neither church, ministry, nor work can exist as a thing by itself. Each has to derive its existence from, find its place in, and work for the good of the Body. All three are from the Body, in the Body, and for the Body. If this principle of relatedness to the Body and interrelatedness among its members is not recognized, there can be no church, no ministry, and no work. The importance of this principle cannot be over-emphasized, for without it everything is man-made, not God-created. The basic principle of the ministry is the Body. The basic principle of the work is the Body. The basic principle of the churches is the Body. The Body is the governing law of the life and work of the children of God today. (*The Normal Christian Church Life*, pp. 187-188)

Further Reading: The Normal Christian Church Life, ch. 9; *Elders' Training, Book 10: The Eldership and the God-ordained Way (2)*, ch. 1; *The Practical Points concerning Blending*, ch. 4

Enlightenment and inspiration: _____

_____

_____

_____

Morning Nourishment

John 1:14 And the Word became flesh...
1 Cor. 15:45 ...The last Adam *became* a life-giving Spirit.
Rev. 1:4 ...Grace to you and peace from Him who is
and who was and who is coming, and from
the seven Spirits who are before His throne.

The New Testament clearly shows us that our Lord became something three times. First, as God, He became flesh; that is, as the infinite God, He became a finite man. Next, as the last Adam, a man in the flesh, He became the life-giving Spirit. Third, as the life-giving Spirit, the pneumatic Christ, He became the seven Spirits. In the New Testament we see that Christ has these three stages. The majority of Christians have seen only one age, the age of the New Testament; they have not seen that within this one age there are three stages. In the first stage He was the Son of Man in the flesh; this is the stage of His incarnation in the four Gospels. In the second stage He is altogether the Spirit; this is the stage of His inclusion from Acts to Jude, the twenty-two books dealing with the life-giving Spirit. In the third stage the life-giving Spirit has become the seven Spirits, the sevenfold intensified Spirit; this is the stage of His intensification in Revelation. These are Christ's three "becomings" in His three stages. His first becoming is in the stage of His incarnation, His second becoming is in the stage of His inclusion, and His third becoming is in the stage of His intensification. This is the New Testament. (*How to Be a Co-worker and an Elder and How to Fulfill Their Obligations,* p. 61)

Today's Reading

In the first stage, the stage of Christ in the flesh, Christ produced a group of redeemed persons, such as Peter and all the other disciples. Although a redeemed people had been produced, the church had not yet been produced. The church was produced by Christ in the second stage. In this stage Christ is the pneumatic Christ, the compound, life-giving Spirit who produced the church on the day of Pentecost. The redeemed saints, who were produced by Christ in the flesh, became the church produced by Christ as the life-giving Spirit.

Shortly after the church was produced, it began to become degraded. This is clearly seen in Acts....Eventually the church degraded to such an extent that the Lord could no longer tolerate it, and He reacted by intensifying Himself sevenfold to become the sevenfold intensified Spirit (Rev. 1:4; 5:6). He became intensified sevenfold to deal with the degradation of the church.

In his Epistles Paul spoke about the Body (Rom. 12:5; 1 Cor. 12:12, 27; Eph. 1:23; 4:4, 16; Col. 2:19), but I do not believe that Paul saw the actual building up of the Body. Paul could see the church expressed in various localities, but he could not see, in actuality, the church as the Body in a perfect and complete way. In order for the Body to be produced in a full and complete way, there is the need of the third stage of Christ, the stage of intensification in which Christ becomes the sevenfold intensified Spirit.

After Paul died, the Lord waited more than twenty years until John wrote the book of Revelation. Revelation is an Epistle, but it is very different in character from all the other Epistles in the New Testament. In this book Christ, who became the compound, all-inclusive, life-giving Spirit, has become the sevenfold intensified Spirit. In Revelation 1:4 the third of the Divine Trinity, the Spirit, becomes the seven Spirits and is ranked as the second of the Divine Trinity.

In His second stage, the stage of His being the compound, all-inclusive, life-giving Spirit, Christ has produced the churches, but not much of the Body was produced and built up in an actual and practical way. For this reason, Christ has become the sevenfold intensified Spirit to overcome the degradation of the church that the overcomers may be produced to bring forth the Body. (*Incarnation, Inclusion, and Intensification*, pp. 18-19)

Further Reading: How to Be a Co-worker and an Elder and How to Fulfill Their Obligations, chs. 1-4; Incarnation, Inclusion, and Intensification, chs. 1-2

Enlightenment and inspiration: _____

_____

_____

Morning Nourishment

Rev. And to the messenger of the church in Sardis write:
3:1 These things says He who has the seven Spirits of
God...
4:5 ...And *there were* seven lamps of fire burning before
the throne, which are the seven Spirits of God.
21:2 And I saw the holy city, New Jerusalem, coming
down out of heaven from God, prepared as a bride
adorned for her husband.

From the foregoing we can see the history of Christ in three
stages: incarnation, inclusion, and intensification. In the first
stage—incarnation—Christ was the Christ in the flesh. In the
second stage—inclusion—Christ is the pneumatic Christ, the
life-giving Spirit. Now in the third stage—intensification—
Christ is the sevenfold intensified Spirit. We need to know
Christ in all three stages. If we know the three stages of incarnation, inclusion, and intensification, we will truly know the Bible.
(*Incarnation, Inclusion, and Intensification*, p. 11)

Today's Reading

I am burdened that all the co-workers in the Lord's recovery
would realize that we need to do a work of three sections. We
should not only be able to do the work of the first section, the section of incarnation, to produce redeemed people, but we should
also be able to do a work that can serve the purpose of the second
section, the section of inclusion, to produce churches. Furthermore, we should be able to do a work to build up the Body of
Christ consummating the New Jerusalem. This is the work of
the stage of intensification.

The first stage—incarnation—is in the physical realm for the
accomplishment of judicial redemption, which is a physical matter. The second stage—inclusion—is divine and mystical. In the
third stage—intensification—there will be a maturing and a
ripening in the divine and mystical realm, and the Body will be
built up to consummate the New Jerusalem.

In releasing this message, I am concerned that the

co-workers are not carrying out a threefold work: the work in the stage of incarnation, the work in the stage of inclusion, and the work in the stage of intensification. If we are carrying out this threefold work, we will work not only to produce redeemed ones and work to establish churches but will also work to build up the Body consummating the New Jerusalem.

I would ask the co-workers to consider what kind of work they have done in the past and ask themselves if they have been doing a work of three sections. Regarding my own work I can say that the work which I did in mainland China was mainly to produce redeemed people. Only a small part of my work there was for the producing of churches. This indicates that my work in China was mainly a work in the first stage. However, when I came to Taiwan, I began to do a work in the stage of inclusion, and many churches were raised up. Now I am burdened to carry out a work in the stage of intensification. Therefore, I pray to the Lord, saying, "Lord, I am endeavoring to do my best to be an overcomer for the building up of Your Body to consummate the New Jerusalem."

I hope that all the co-workers will see the three stages, the three sections, of Christ: incarnation—the stage of Christ in the flesh; inclusion—the stage of Christ as the life-giving Spirit; and intensification—the stage of Christ as the sevenfold intensified life-giving Spirit. These three stages are the three sections of Christ's history. This means that Christ's history is divided into the section of His incarnation, the section of His inclusion, and the section of His intensification. Therefore we emphasize these three words—*incarnation, inclusion,* and *intensification*—and stress the facts that incarnation produces redeemed people, that inclusion produces the churches, and that intensification produces the overcomers to build up the Body, which consummates in the New Jerusalem as the unique goal of God's economy. This is the revelation in the New Testament. (*Incarnation, Inclusion, and Intensification,* pp. 20-21)

Further Reading: Incarnation, Inclusion, and Intensification, chs. 1-2

Enlightenment and inspiration: _____

_____

_____

_____

Morning Nourishment

Rev. And I saw...a Lamb standing as having *just* been
5:6 slain, having seven horns and seven eyes, which are
the seven Spirits of God sent forth into all the earth.

1 Cor. I planted, Apollos watered, but God caused the
3:6, 9 growth....For we are God's fellow workers; you are
God's cultivated land, God's building.

16:10 Now if Timothy comes, see that he is with you without fear; for he is working the work of the Lord,
even as I am.

My use of the word *inclusion* is based on our use of the word *in-clusive*. For the last Adam to become the life-giving Spirit was for Christ to become the all-inclusive Spirit. His becoming all-inclusive was a matter not just of incarnation but of inclusion....In the stage of inclusion, many things are included in the pneumatic Christ, in the Christ who is the life-giving Spirit. Now we need to see that the all-inclusive, life-giving Spirit has been intensified sevenfold.

I would urge you to consider this matter of intensification and to pray desperately, saying, "Lord, I must advance. I need Your grace to bring me onward. I do not want to remain in the work of incarnation nor even in the work of inclusion. I want to advance from inclusion to intensification. Lord, You have been intensified sevenfold, and I pray that I also will be intensified sevenfold to overcome the degradation of the church that the Body may be built up to consummate the New Jerusalem." (*Incarnation, Inclusion, and Intensification*, p. 22)

Today's Reading

What kind of work should we be doing today? We should be do-ing a work of all three sections. I am concerned that many of the co-workers are still working only in the first section, the section of incarnation. If this is your situation, you need to improve and to ad-vance. What you have learned and what you have done in the past are not adequate. Of course, you should not discard the things of the first stage, for those things are the foundation. Now you need to begin building on this foundation and eventually have the completion of the building. The foundation is the work in the stage of incarnation; the building up is the work in the stage of inclusion; and the completion of the building is the work in the stage of intensification. (*Incarnation, Inclusion, and Intensification*, p. 21)

Today there are four kinds of workers. The first are the co-workers who match the need of the ministry of God in the present age. This is a small group of people who have been dealt with by the Lord and who are in one accord. The second kind are the younger co-workers. They are willing to receive the direction and to come under the coordination of the older co-workers, and they are willing to follow and to learn in humility. The third kind are those who are unwilling to submit to the senior co-workers, who do not belong to the denominations, yet who are happy to remain in fellowship with us. The fourth kind are the preachers and free evangelists among the denominations. What we need today are the first and the second kind of co-workers.

When a co-worker is in a certain place, he has to cooperate with the local church in that place. The work and the church cannot be separated one from the other. When a co-worker is working in a certain place, he is at the same time one of the local brothers. When the church assigns work to the saints, the co-workers should stand on the same ground as the local brothers and should accept assignments in the same way.

Concerning the third and the fourth kind of co-workers, we can only let them choose their own pathway. With some people, God has not assigned them to take the same way as we do, and we dare not say anything to them. Whatever the situation may be, we are here to do the work that God has committed to us. We cannot interfere with others' work, and we are not here tearing down others' work. (*Messages Given during the Resumption of Watchman Nee's Ministry*, pp. 147-148)

Further Reading: Incarnation, Inclusion, and Intensification, chs. 1-2; *Messages Given during the Resumption of Watchman Nee's Ministry,* ch. 26

Enlightenment and inspiration: _____

_____

_____

_____

Hymns, #913

1   Serve and work within the Body,
     This the Lord doth signify;
  For His purpose is the Body,
     And with it we must comply.

     Serve and work within the Body,
       Never independently;
     As the members of the Body,
       Functioning relatedly.

2   As the members we've been quickened
     Not as individuals free;
  We must always serve together,
     All related mutually.

3   Living stones, we're built together
     And a house for God must be,
  As the holy priesthood serving,
     In a blessed harmony.

4   Thus we must be built together,
     In position minister;
  For the basis of our service
     Is the body character.

5   In our ministry and service,
     From the Body, our supply;
  If detached and isolated,
     Out of function we will die.

6   'Tis by serving in the Body
     Riches of the Head we share;
  'Tis by functioning as members
     Christ's full measure we will bear.

7   To the Head fast holding ever,
     That we may together grow,
  From the Head supplies incoming
     Thru us to the Body flow.

8   Lord, anew we give our bodies;
     May we be transformed to prove
  All Thy will, to know Thy Body,
     And therein to serve and move.

Composition for prophecy with main point and sub-points: _____

_____
_____
_____
_____
_____
_____
_____
_____
_____
_____
_____
_____
_____
_____
_____
_____
_____
_____
_____
_____
_____
_____
_____
_____
_____
_____
_____
_____
_____
_____
_____
_____
_____
_____
_____

God's Building

Scripture Reading: Matt. 16:18; Eph. 2:21-22; 3:17a; 4:16; 1 Pet. 2:5; Rev. 21:2

Day 1   I. The main subject of the Bible is God's building; thus, the entire Bible is a book of building (Gen. 2:22; 28:10-22; Matt. 16:18; Eph. 4:16; Rev. 21:2).

II. The central and divine thought of the Scriptures is that God is seeking a divine building as the mingling of Himself with humanity; He is seeking a living composition of living persons redeemed by and mingled with Himself (John 14:20; 1 John 4:15):

A. The principle of God's building is that God builds Himself into man and builds man into Himself; God mingling with man is God building Himself into man, and man mingling with God is man being built into God (Eph. 3:17a).

B. God intends to have a building in which God is built into man and man is built into God so that God and man, man and God, can be a mutual abode to each other (John 15:4a; Rev. 21:2-3, 22).

Day 2 & Day 3 III. God's building is the corporate expression of the Triune God (1 Tim. 3:15-16; John 17:22; Eph. 3:19b, 21):

A. God's intention is to have a group of people built up as a spiritual building to express God and to represent God by dealing with His enemy and recovering the lost earth (Gen. 1:26; 1 Pet. 2:5, 9).

B. The building up of the saints into one corporate expression is the real testimony (Rev. 1:2, 12, 20).

IV. God's building is the enlargement of God (John 3:29a, 30a; Col. 2:19):

A. The proper building is the enlargement, the expansion, of the Triune God, enabling God to express Himself in a corporate way (Eph. 2:21-22; Col. 2:19).

B. The building of God is the Triune God as life being wrought into us so that we may become His one expression, the enlargement and expansion of God (Eph. 3:17a, 19b, 21).

Day 4   V. **To be built up with fellow believers is the Lord's supreme and highest requirement of His faithful seekers according to one of the divine attributes—the divine oneness (John 17).**

VI. **The prerequisites of the believers' being built up in the church, the Body of Christ, include:**

A. Realizing that the Lord, according to the desire of His heart, wants a built church (Matt. 16:18).

B. Being in harmony with the fellow believers and being in one accord with the Body in prayer (18:19; Acts 1:14).

C. Practicing the oneness of the Divine Trinity in the Divine Trinity as the Divine Trinity does (John 17:21-23).

D. Keeping the oneness of the Spirit in the constitution of the Body with the Divine Trinity (Eph. 4:3-6).

E. Being in the common fellowship of the enjoyment of Christ and having the common thinking and love in one spirit, with one soul (1 Cor. 1:2, 9; Phil. 2:1-2; 1:27).

F. Living and walking by the Spirit and walking by the mingled spirit (Gal. 5:16, 25; Rom. 8:4).

G. Being conformed to the death of Christ and magnifying Christ (Phil. 3:10; 1:19-21).

Day 5 VII. **The book of Ezekiel begins with a vision of the appearance of the glory of the Lord (1:4-28) and ends with a vision of the holy building of God; this indicates that God's goal is the building and that the glory of the Lord, the judgment of God, and the recovery of the Lord are all for the holy building of God (40:1—48:35):**

A. In Ezekiel 40—48, a section on God's building,

three main things are covered: the holy temple, the Holy Land, and the holy city:

1. The recovery of the land signifies the recovery of the experience and enjoyment of the riches of Christ.
2. The temple is God's house for His rest, and the city is God's kingdom for His authority (48:35b).

B. Ezekiel saw the glory of the Lord coming back to the house of the Lord; the glory could return only after the building of the temple was completed (44:4).

C. "This is the place of My throne and the place of the soles of My feet, where I will dwell in the midst of the children of Israel forever" (43:7a):

1. The Lord's throne is for His administration, and the soles of the Lord's feet are for His move on earth.
2. Apart from the temple as the place of His throne and the place of the soles of His feet, the Lord has no base for His administration and for His move.

Day 6

D. The Lord instructed Ezekiel to describe God's house (40:4; 43:10-12):

1. God's intention was to check the living and conduct of His people by the house; in the book of Ezekiel, God measured them by the temple:

   a. Because the house of God was to be their regulation, God charged Ezekiel to show them the form of the house.
   b. The temple of God is a pattern, and if the people examine themselves in light of this pattern, they will know their shortcomings (v. 11; 41:16-20).
   c. The living of the people must match the temple of God (1 Cor. 3:16-17).

2. According to the book of Ezekiel the requirements of the indwelling Christ are

according to His house; everyone must be
measured and checked according to the
measurement of God's house (43:10):

a. Our behavior and conduct should be examined not only according to moral regulations and spiritual principles but also
   according to the church, the house of God
   (1 Tim. 3:15-16).

b. Our main concern should not be with be-
   having ourselves or with becoming spiritual but with fitting into God's house
   (1 Cor. 14:12).

c. If what we are and what we do cannot
   match God's building, it amounts to
   nothing in the sight of God (3:10-15).

Morning Nourishment

Matt. **...I will build My church, and the gates of Hades**
16:18 **shall not prevail against it.**
John **In that day you will know that I am in My Father,**
14:20 **and you in Me, and I in you.**
  15:4 **Abide in Me and I in you....**

The principle of the Lord being a building is that God mingles Himself with humanity, and this is the principle of God's building in general. Therefore, the church also is the divine mingling of God Himself with humanity. The church is not something of the old creation. It is God's building composed of God Himself as the divine material mingled with man as the human material. In this sense, the church is a hybrid. A hybrid is a mingling of two lives and natures into one entity....The church is a divine hybrid as the mingling of God with man.

We may speak much concerning the building of the church, but we must realize that the building is the mingling of God with man. The more we are mingled with God, the more we are built up together. It is impossible for us to be built up together without God. Even if we could be built in this way, that would not be the building of God; it would merely be a building of people. The church as the building of God is not a combination or composition of humans. Rather, it is a mingling of God with humanity. (*The Building of God*, pp. 10-11)

Today's Reading

The central and divine thought of the Scriptures is that God is seeking a divine building as the mingling of Himself with humanity. He is seeking a living composition of living persons redeemed by and mingled with Himself.

Today God is doing the work of the divine building, which is to mingle Himself with man. We preach the gospel not merely to win souls or save souls from hell but to minister God Himself through the Spirit to man so that God can be mingled with man. In this way we gain the materials for the divine building. Likewise, we minister Christ to the saints so that they can be mingled and built up together with Christ. This is the basic and central thought behind what we do.

The success of a ministry is in ministering Christ into people and helping them to mingle with Christ. Before we come under such a ministry, we may have only a little of Christ, but after we come, we gain much Christ. This ministry ministers Christ to us, helps us to grow in Christ, and mingles us with Christ all the time. This carries out the building, which is the divine mingling of God Himself with man.

To be mingled with God day by day is a deep, basic, and central matter. Husbands should love their wives, and wives should submit to their husbands, but for husbands merely to love their wives means little. The real love that is worthy before God is the love that is a mingling of Christ with the husbands. If Christ is mingled in the love of a person, there is the divine building. [For a wife]…simply to submit to a husband means little. The submission of the wives should be something of Christ mingled with them. If there is something of Christ mingled with a wife's submission, there is the divine building. Both the love of the husbands and the submission of the wives must be the mingling of Christ with man, that is, the divine building.

After His work of creation, God's work of building is to mingle Himself with man. In every spiritual experience, God must be mingled with us as the divine building. It is not sufficient to be humble or to love and submit. There must be the divine building, which is the mingling of God within. By this word we can now understand what the building of God, the house of God, and the dwelling of God are. The dwelling place of God is the mingling of God with man. This is also the building of the church. By the grace of God, may we more and more see the mingling of God with man as the real, divine building. (*The Building of God*, pp. 13-14)

Further Reading: The Building of God, ch. 1; Life and Building as Portrayed in the Song of Songs, chs. 1, 8-9, 12, 15-16; Life-study of Exodus, msgs. 116-117

Enlightenment and inspiration: _____

_____

_____

_____

Morning Nourishment

Gen. And God said, Let Us make man in Our image, accord-
1:26 ing to Our likeness; and let them have dominion...
1 Tim. But if I delay, I *write* that you may know how one
3:15-16 ought to conduct himself in the house of God, which
is the church of the living God, the pillar and base of
the truth. And confessedly, great is the mystery of
godliness: He who was manifested in the flesh...
Rev. And I saw the holy city, New Jerusalem, coming
21:2 down out of heaven from God, prepared as a bride
adorned for her husband.

God has only *one* image, and since His image is one, He can only
have one expression. There are many thousands of Christians on
this earth. How then can so many be just *one* expression of God?
The answer is in God's building! We must have the building. I do
not have words to express what is on my heart concerning this
matter. There is a vision open to me continuously day and night.
First, negatively, it is impossible for any single individual to express God in a full way; then, positively, the proper and adequate
expression of God must be a coordinated, corporate expression. Remember, God's desire and purpose is that He be expressed and represented through man on this earth. But this is possible only when
we are being mutually coordinated and built up together. Then
God will be fully expressed. Oh, we must be built up with other
Christians as a corporate expression, representing God! God's first
created man failed to be His one expression, but the principle still
holds: the other man created by God—the new man—is to be that
all-inclusive, corporate man, God's real expression on this earth.
(*The Vision of God's Building,* pp. 14-15)

Today's Reading

Let us be more practical. Christians talk much about being like
Jesus, glorifying God, and expressing Christ. But it is impossible
for any *individual* to glorify God or express Christ in a *full way* if he
is not *built up* with other Christians. Consider ourselves. All of our
problems are due to one thing: we are too independent and

individualistic; we are disconnected and isolated from others. So we are beset with failures and weaknesses. Do you have a certain besetting sin which you cannot overcome? You will never surmount it or overcome it by yourself. You must forget your own efforts and pay full attention to being built up with others. If we are willing to be vitally related and built up with others, we will find that our weaknesses and shortcomings will disappear. We must learn to pay attention to one thing: being built up with other Christians. In the early years of my Christian life I did not see this building principle. I was struggling and striving, seeking and fighting. One day the Lord opened my eyes. I saw that there was no need for me to struggle, fight and toil any longer. I need only abide in the Body. As long as each member of my physical body abides in the body, everything is all right.

Suppose your hand is isolated and separated from your body; yet it continues with great effort to live and function, to be healthy and useful! Suppose someone should ask the severed hand, "What are you striving for...?" and it replies, "Oh, I must strive to be healthy, to overcome all the germs, etc., etc." Such a supposition is absurd in the extreme. Yet this is the case of most Christians today, probably including yourself. Yes, we are Christians, but we are not *actually* related to one another. We are members of Christ's Body, but we are not *fitly framed* together. We are materials, but we are not *built up* together as God's building. Oh, we must forget our personal struggles and just abide in the Body!...Let us forget our striving and just pay attention to being vitally related to Christ's Body. Then the germs will be killed, and we will be living and powerful, healthy and functioning. We will not merely be useful, but *fully* useful.

At the end of Scripture, as its conclusion, there is one city. And this city is the building, the unique, universal expression of God. God always has only *one* expression. As in Genesis 1, there is only one man, so at the end of Scripture there is only one city, built of gold, pearls and precious stones. (*The Vision of God's Building*, pp. 15-16)

Further Reading: The Vision of God's Building, chs. 1-4

Enlightenment and inspiration: _____

_____

_____

_____

Morning Nourishment

John   He who has the bride is the bridegroom....He must
3:29-30 increase...
   Col.   And not holding the Head, out from whom all the
   2:19   Body, being richly supplied and knit together by
           means of the joints and sinews, grows with the
           growth of God.
   Eph.   That Christ may make His home in your hearts...
3:17, 19 that you may be filled unto all the fullness of God.

As Christians, can we point out other definite members of the Body of Christ with whom we are related in a practical way? This is not a matter of doctrine or ethereal "spirituality"; it is a matter of practical reality. Check yourself. If you are an isolated member of the Body, you are burdened with many problems. The only way to be a victorious Christian is to be a related Christian. When we come to the Body, we find that all the besetting sins are under our feet! The issue is not whether we are a living, healthy, or functioning, *individual* Christian; but are we vitally and practically related to the Body of Christ? It is a pity, but it is a fact that very little is heard today regarding the building of God and the real relatedness of the Body of Christ on this earth. I do hope that we all may see that it is God's intention to have a corporate man as a building, a unique expression, with so many members fitly framed together, members related and built up as one Body. Then, wherever we are, we will enjoy all the riches of the Body. (*The Vision of God's Building,* pp. 16-17)

Today's Reading

Building is actually the enlargement of God. Building is the enlargement of God to express God in a corporate way. We have seen that life is God Himself wrought into our being. If the Triune God has truly been wrought into us, the issue will be an enlargement and an expansion of God. As I have mentioned earlier in this message, God did not create a couple; He only created a man. The wife came out of the husband, becoming the enlargement of her husband. That was building. Eve, as the wife of

Adam, was God's building, and that building was the enlargement of Adam. Adam was a figure and type of God becoming a man, and Eve was a figure and type of God's building. Since this building was a part of Adam, it was undoubtedly his enlargement and expansion.

We need to read the Bible carefully. In Genesis 1 God was alone. At the end of the book of Revelation, God is in the center of the holy city, New Jerusalem, which is His enlargement. In the beginning we find God Himself without any expansion or enlargement. However, throughout the ages and generations God has been working Himself into His chosen people. Eventually we all shall become His building, a building which is the enlargement of God Himself. Hence, this building will become God's expansion, and this expansion will express God in a corporate way. This is God's building. Building is not simply that I depend upon you, that you depend upon me, and that the brothers and sisters depend upon one another. That is not an adequate understanding of building. The proper building is the enlargement of God, the expansion of the Triune God, enabling God to express Himself in a corporate way. This is exactly the revelation of the Gospel of John. The Gospel of John reveals that the Triune God is dispensing Himself into His believers and that all His believers, as a result of the transfusion and infusion of the Triune God into them, become His enlargement. This enlargement of the Triune God is the expansion, the building, and the expression of God. This is the revelation of the Gospel of John. Thus, when we speak of the building of God, we mean that the Triune God as life is being wrought into us continually and that under His transfusion and infusion we are becoming His one expression. This expression is His enlargement and expansion. May this thought be written on our heart. (*Life-study of John*, pp. 5-6)

Further Reading: The Vision of God's Building, ch. 1; Life-study of John, msgs. 1, 4-5

Enlightenment and inspiration: _____

_____

_____

_____

Morning Nourishment

John 17:21-23   **That they all may be one; even as You, Father, are in Me and I in You, that they also may be in Us; that the world may believe that You have sent Me. And the glory which You have given Me I have given to them, that they may be one, even as We are one; I in them, and You in Me, that they may be perfected into one...**

To be built up with the fellow believers is the Lord's supreme and highest requirement to His faithful seekers according to one of the divine attributes of the Divine Trinity (John 17). Our oneness, to which we testify in the Lord's table meeting, is according to the divine oneness, which is an attribute of the Divine Trinity.

Being built up with the fellow partakers of the divine life is the highest virtue of the one who pursues after Christ in God's eternal economy. Building is the highest requirement, and being built up is the highest virtue. (*The Secret of God's Organic Salvation: "The Spirit Himself with Our Spirit,"* p. 51)

Today's Reading

There are many prerequisites of the believers' building up in the church, the Body of Christ.

The first prerequisite is to realize that the Lord loves and wants to have, according to the desire of His heart, His good pleasure, a built church, not scattered individual believers. If we are scattered individuals, we can have no part in the building up of the church. It is crucial for us to see this.

Another prerequisite is that we acknowledge that all the believers have been baptized in one Spirit into one Body and that God has placed the members in the Body and blended all the Body together (1 Cor. 12:13a, 18, 24).

We also need to be in harmony with the fellow believers and to be in one accord with the Body in prayer, which issues in the establishment of the church (Matt. 18:19; Acts 1:14).

The believers need to practice the oneness of the Divine Trinity in the Divine Trinity as the Divine Trinity does (John 17:21-23)....

Some claim to be practicing the oneness of the Body, but they are

actually practicing a sectarian, factious oneness. The oneness of the
Body is the oneness of the Triune God. We practice the oneness of the
Divine Trinity not in ourselves but in the Divine Trinity. The three of
the Divine Trinity…are continually practicing the divine oneness.

The next prerequisite is to keep the oneness of the Spirit dili-
gently (Eph. 4:3). We keep this oneness in the constitution of the
Body with the Divine Trinity (4:4-6) as the source (the Father), the
element (the Son), and the essence (the Spirit). We also keep this
oneness through the perfection by the gifted members for the building up of the Body of Christ (vv. 11-12). This means that keeping the
oneness is related not only to the Triune God but also to the gifted
persons—the apostles, the prophets, the evangelists, and the shepherds and teachers. Moreover, we keep the oneness by the growth
in the divine life, growing into the Head in all things (vv. 13, 15).

The believers also need to be in the common fellowship of the
enjoyment of Christ as the believers' common portion for the
keeping of the oneness of the Body to witness that Christ is neither divisible nor divided (1 Cor. 1:2, 9-13).

Another prerequisite is that the believers have the common
fellowship in the spirit and have the common thinking and common love in one spirit, with one soul, and on one common standing for the testimony of the oneness of the Body of Christ (Phil.
2:1-2; 1:27). If you have fellowship only in your district, that is not
common fellowship but a particular fellowship. The common fellowship is universal. Our fellowship, therefore, must be universal.

Next, the believers should live and walk by the Spirit (Gal.
5:16, 25) and walk according to the mingled spirit (Rom. 8:4), set-
ting their mind on the mingled spirit, which is indwelt by the
pneumatic Christ, the indwelling Spirit, to impart life within
them and for them to put to death the practices of the body (Rom.
8:4, 6, 9-13). (*The Secret of God's Organic Salvation: "The Spirit
Himself with Our Spirit,"* pp. 52-55)

*Further Reading: The Secret of God's Organic Salvation: "The Spirit
Himself with Our Spirit,"* ch. 4

Enlightenment and inspiration: _____

_____
_____
_____

Morning Nourishment

Ezek. Then He brought me through the north gate to the
44:4 front of the house; and I looked, and just then the
glory of Jehovah filled the house of Jehovah, and I
fell upon my face.
43:5 And the Spirit took me up and brought me into the
inner court, and just then the glory of Jehovah
filled the house.
    7 And He said to me, Son of man, *this is* the place of
My throne and the place of the soles of My feet,
where I will dwell in the midst of the children of
Israel forever....

It is important for us to understand why the glory of the
Lord came back [in Ezekiel 43]. The glory of the Lord returned
because the building of the temple was completed. This is the
crucial point. How much the Lord desires to come back to the
earth! Yet, for His coming back He needs a place for the soles
of His feet to rest, a place upon which He can set His feet. His
habitation, His house, is the place on earth where He can put
His feet.

We need to be deeply impressed with the fact that the glory
of God returned only after the building of the temple was completed. If we want to dwell in the church and manifest His
glory in the church, the church must be complete. If the
church today corresponds to all the details of the holy building
of God covered in Ezekiel 40—48 and thus is built up in every
aspect, God will dwell in the church gloriously. Therefore, in
order for the glorious God to dwell in the church, the church
must be built up to become the dwelling place of God.
(*Life-study of Ezekiel,* pp. 273, 275)

Today's Reading

[In Ezekiel 43:5] we see that the Lord has returned to the
earth. Because He had lost His standing on earth, He went
back to the heavens. The Lord's standing on earth is the

building up of His house. In order for the Lord to come back to the earth, He needs a built up church as His standing on the earth. The Lord will not simply come back to the earth; the Lord will come back to the church.

At the time Ezekiel saw the glory of the Lord, he also saw a man standing by him. He saw both the glory of the Lord and the Lord as a man. The man who stood by him said, "Son of man, this is the place of My throne and the place of the soles of My feet, where I will dwell in the midst of the children of Israel forever" (v. 7a). The words *the place of my throne* prove that the man who stood by Ezekiel was the Lord Himself.

Here we see the Lord's desire for His house, for the church. The Lord cares for the recovery of the church life. He has been desiring and waiting to come back to the church. This is why we have so much joy in the meetings. We are joyful and happy because the Lord within us is joyful and happy. He is happy because in the church He has a place—a place for His throne, a place for the soles of His feet. For centuries the Lord did not have on earth a place for the soles of His feet. How happy He is that, having been kept away from the earth for so long, He now has the local churches as the place of His throne and the place of the soles of His feet!

The place of the soles of the Lord's feet is the place of His throne. The throne is for God's government, administration, and kingdom; it is the place from which He can administrate. The soles of the Lord's feet are for His move on earth. Apart from the temple as the place of His throne and the place of the soles of His feet, the Lord has no base for His administration and move on the earth. Unless the church is built up, the Lord has no standing to administrate His government and to move on the earth. Furthermore, the church is the place where the Lord can dwell for His rest and satisfaction. (*Life-study of Ezekiel,* pp. 277-279)

Further Reading: Life-study of Ezekiel, msgs. 19-27

Enlightenment and inspiration: _____

_____

_____

_____

Morning Nourishment

Ezek. You, O son of man, describe the house to the house of
43:10-11 Israel, that they may feel humiliated because of their
iniquities, and let them measure the pattern....Make
known to them the design of the house, the arrangement, its exits, its entrances, its whole design, and all
its statutes—indeed its whole design and all its laws;
and write *them* down in their sight, that they may
keep its whole design and all its statutes, and do them.
1 Tim. But if I delay, I write that you may know how one
3:15 ought to conduct himself in the house of God, which
is the church of the living God...

[In Ezekiel 43:10-11], the Lord did not charge Ezekiel to teach
God's people the law and the Ten Commandments as He had
charged Moses. Rather, He told Ezekiel to show God's house to the
people. Here the Lord seemed to be saying, "From now on, it is a
matter not of the dispensation of the law but of the dispensation
of My house. Simply to keep the law is not good enough. You have
to keep the form, the fashion, the ordinances, the statutes, the
laws, the comings in, and the goings out related to the house. You
should behave not merely according to the Ten Commandments
but also according to My house."

God wanted Ezekiel to show the temple to the house of Israel
so that the people would be ashamed of their iniquities. The
temple of God is a pattern, and if the people would examine themselves in light of this pattern, they would know their shortcomings. It was God's intention to check the living and conduct of the
people of Israel by His house, His habitation, as a rule and pattern. The living of the people of God must match the temple of
God. Showing the temple to God's people exposes their sins and
shortcomings and causes them to be ashamed of their iniquities.
(*Life-study of Ezekiel*, p. 280)

Today's Reading

Most believers today feel that moral regulations and spiritual
principles are sufficient as rules of behavior and conduct. Few

realize that our behavior and conduct should be examined not only according to moral regulations and spiritual principles but also according to the church, the house of God.

Suppose a certain young man gets saved. Before he was saved, he treated his parents and his sister quite poorly. Now that he has been saved, he learns how to treat them with respect and to behave rightly and properly....Later, he learns to be spiritual....He is good in conduct and in certain matters he is even spiritual; however, he is altogether independent. He is so independent that he is not willing to pray with others. Such a person...does not know anything about God's house. He does not care at all for the church. Everything he does is for himself individually; nothing is for the church, the Body, Christ's corporate expression.

Today the Lord's concern is not the law—it is the house. His concern is not spirituality—it is the church....Because the Lord cares so much for the church, His house, we also should care for the church as His house and fashion ourselves according to it. If we realize this, we will...care absolutely for the church and fashion ourselves according to the church, God's house.

The church life...is the greatest test of real spirituality. If we cannot pass the test of the church life, our spirituality is not genuine.

We need to see from the book of Ezekiel that the requirement of the indwelling Christ is not according to the law but according to His house. Everyone must be measured and checked according to the measurement of God's house. We are not under the dispensation of the law; we are under the dispensation of the house. This is the age of the church, not the age merely of being spiritual. Now is the time for the church life. If what we are and what we do cannot fit into the church life, it amounts to nothing in the sight of God and may even be an abomination to Him, a kind of whoredom. Therefore, we need to fashion ourselves according to the church and allow the church to measure us and check us in every aspect. (*Life-study of Ezekiel*, pp. 280-284)

Further Reading: Life-study of Ezekiel, msg. 24

Enlightenment and inspiration: What a shame it is and would be to be "spiritual" and miss this great revelation of the church life!

Hymns, #839

1 Lord, Thou art a potter skilled
And a glorious builder too,
Molding for Thy vessel great,
Building with Thy house in view.
I am both a man of clay
And a new-made living stone,
That Thy vessel I may be
And the temple Thou wouldst own.

2 Though of clay Thou madest us,
Thou wouldst have us be transformed;
With Thy life as purest gold,
Unto precious stones conformed.
We shall, through Thy building work,
Then become Thy loving Bride,
In one Body joined to Thee,
That Thy heart be satisfied.

3 What Thy heart desires and loves
Are not precious stones alone,
But together these to build
For Thy glory, for Thy home.
Thou, the all-inclusive Christ,
Dost a builded Church require,
That Thy glorious riches may
Radiate their light entire.

4 Not the person spiritual
In an individual way,
But the corporate life expressed
Will Thy heart's desire display.
Members separate and detached
Ne'er express Thee perfectly,
But Thy Body tempered, built,
Ever shall Thy fulness be.

5 Build me, Lord, with other saints,
Independence ne'er allow,
But according to Thy plan
Fitly frame and join me now.
In experience not my boast,
Nor in gifts would be my pride;
For Thy building I give all,
That Thou may be glorified.

*Composition for prophecy with main point and
sub-points:* _____

_____
_____
_____
_____
_____
_____
_____
_____
_____
_____
_____
_____
_____
_____
_____
_____
_____
_____
_____
_____
_____
_____
_____
_____
_____
_____
_____
_____
_____
_____
_____
_____
_____
_____
_____
_____
_____

The Recovery of the Israel of God

Scripture Reading: Gal. 6:15-16; 3:6-9, 14, 29; 4:28, 31; 5:16-18, 22-23, 25; 6:8

Day 1 & Day 2

I. **There is the need for the Lord to recover the real Israel of God (6:16):**

A. God's New Testament economy is not only to make us sons of God but also to make us the Israel of God (Eph. 1:5; Heb. 2:10; Rom. 8:14, 19; Gal. 3:26; 4:6-7; 6:16).

B. Today we need to be such an Israel, a prince, to execute God's government on earth (Matt. 6:9-10).

II. **The apostle Paul considers the many individual believers in Christ collectively the Israel of God (Gal. 6:8, 16):**

A. The Israel of God is the real Israel including all the Gentile and Jewish believers in Christ, who are the true sons of Abraham, who are the household of the faith, and who are those in the new creation (Rom. 9:6b; 2:28-29; Phil. 3:3; Gal. 6:15-16, 10; 3:7, 29).

B. The real Israel, the spiritual Israel, is the church (6:16; Matt. 16:18).

C. In God's New Testament economy we have been made both the sons of God and the Israel of God (Gal. 3:26; 6:16):

1. We are sons of God, members of God's family, for His expression (v. 10).

2. We are kings-to-be, those destined to be kings; kingship is related to the Israel of God (Rev. 5:10).

3. Our destiny is to be sons of God expressing God and also kings reigning in the kingdom of God (21:7; 22:5b; 12:5a):

a. As the sons of God, the new creation, we need to be loving, joyful, peaceful, faithful, and meek (Gal. 3:26; 5:22-23).

b. As the Israel of God, princes and victors,

we need to walk according to the elementary rules of God's New Testament economy (v. 25; 6:16).

D. Paul's word about the Israel of God implies that we need to live in a kingly way with a kingly walk (Rom. 5:17, 21).

Day 3 **III. As the Israel of God, we represent God, exercise His authority, and carry out His administration on earth for the fulfillment of His purpose (Gen. 1:26, 28; Luke 10:19; Rev. 12:5, 7-11):**

A. God wants His creature man to deal with His creature Satan in order to bring the earth back to God (Psa. 149:7-9).

B. God needs man to do the work of God—to reign over His creation, to proclaim His triumph, and to cause Satan to suffer loss (Gen. 1:26).

C. May God open our eyes to see that His purpose demands that we be wholly and absolutely for Him.

Day 4 **IV. If we would be the Israel of God, we need to experience the God of Abraham, Isaac, and Jacob (Exo. 3:6, 15-16):**

A. "The God of Abraham, the God of Isaac, and the God of Jacob" is Jehovah Elohim, the Triune God—the Father, the Son, and the Spirit (v. 15; Gen. 2:4-22; Matt. 28:19).

B. Abraham, Isaac, and Jacob are the foundations of the nation of Israel; without them there would not be the nation of Israel (Exo. 3:15-16):

1. God's people became His people through the experiences of Abraham, Isaac, and Jacob.

2. The dealings which Abraham, Isaac, and Jacob received before God and the experiences they went through culminated in a people of God.

3. We all need to have the elements of Abraham, Isaac, and Jacob; without these elements we cannot be the people of God, the Israel of God.

C. In the book of Genesis, the record of Abraham, Isaac, and Jacob overlap; Genesis does not portray them as three separate individuals but as constituents of one corporate person:

1. The experience of Abraham signifies the experience of God the Father, the unique source, in His calling man, justifying man, and equipping man to live by faith and to live in fellowship with Him (12:1; 15:6; chs. 17—18; 19:29; 21:1-13; 22:1-18).

2. The experience of Isaac signifies the experience of God the Son in His redeeming man and His blessing man with the inheritance of all His riches, with a life of the enjoyment of His abundance, and with a life in peace (vv. 1-14; 25:5; 26:3-4, 12-33).

3. The experience of Jacob (with Joseph) signifies the experience of God the Father in His loving man and choosing man (Mal. 1:2; Rom. 9:10-13) and of God the Spirit in His working all things for the good of those who love Him, in His transforming man, and in His making man mature in the divine life that man may be able to bless all the people, rule over all the earth, and satisfy all the people with God the Son as the life supply (Gen. 27:41; 28:1—35:15; chs. 37; 39—49; Rom. 8:28-29).

Day 5 V. **In order to be the Israel of God representing God, in Christ we "were circumcised with a circumcision not made with hands, in the putting off of the body of the flesh, in the circumcision of Christ" (Col. 2:11):**

A. The spiritual meaning of circumcision is to put off the flesh, to put off the self and the old man, through the crucifixion of Christ (Gen. 17:10-14; Deut. 10:16; Jer. 4:4a; Rom. 2:28-29).

B. Because we reject our flesh altogether and have no confidence in the flesh, we are the real circumcision (Phil. 3:3).

VI. **There are two kinds of walk by the Spirit, and the second kind of walk constitutes us those who live a new creation and are the Israel of God (Gal. 5:16, 25):**
  A. We need to "walk by this rule"—the rule of being a new creation, of having the Triune God as our life and living (6:15-16).
  B. The meaning of the new creation is that the processed and consummated Triune God mingles Himself with us and constitutes us with Himself to make us new (Eph. 4:4-6, 24; Col. 3:10-11).
  C. To live the new creation is to walk by the divine life and divine nature as a governing principle (Gal. 6:15-16).

Day 6 VII. **Peace reigns upon the real Israel of God, upon those who walk by the rule of living a new creation (vv. 15-16).**

VIII. **Today's Israel of God is a miniature of the coming New Jerusalem, which will be the ultimate consummation of the Israel of God (Rev. 21:2).**

Morning Nourishment

Gal. And as many as walk by this rule, peace be upon
6:16 them and mercy, even upon the Israel of God.
3:26 For you are all sons of God through faith in Christ
Jesus.
5:22-23 But the fruit of the Spirit is love, joy, peace, long-
suffering, kindness, goodness, faithfulness, meekness, self-control; against such things there is no law.
2 Tim. If we endure, we will also reign with *Him*...
2:12

Paul concludes Galatians 6:16 with the words, "even upon the Israel of God." The Greek word rendered "even" (*kai*) here is not connective but explicative, indicating that the apostle considers the many individual believers in Christ collectively the Israel of God. The Israel of God is the real Israel (Rom. 9:6; 2:28-29; Phil. 3:3), including all the Gentile and Jewish believers in Christ. These are the true sons of Abraham (Gal. 3:7, 29), the household of the faith (6:10).

Those who walk by "this rule" are the true Israel, the Israel of God. In a way there is no difference between the nation of Israel and the secular world or the religious world. In the eyes of God, the nation of Israel is not the real Israel. We, the sons of God, are the true Israel, for we are God's household, His chosen people to-day. We may not be Israel outwardly, but we are Israel inwardly. This is why we say that we, the believers in Christ, are the true Israel. The outward nation of Israel has little concern for God. However, we have a genuine concern for God and speak of Him continually. We are indeed the Israel of God. (*Life-study of Galatians*, pp. 269-270)

Today's Reading

As sons of God [Gal. 3:26], we are His folks, members of His household. But God's New Testament economy is not only to make us His sons, but also to make us the Israel of God.

Perhaps we can understand the difference between the sons of God and the Israel of God if we consider as an illustration how a son in a royal family is trained to be king. On the one hand, such a son grows up as a member of the royal family, the son of the king and queen. On the other hand, he must be trained in order to become king in the future. Thus, he must have two kinds of living: the first, as a son in the royal family; the second, as a king-to-be. If he has the first kind of living without the second, he will not become equipped or qualified to be king. A boy is not trained to be a king overnight. Nor does he become qualified to be a king simply by developing certain virtues. If he is joyful, loving, meek, faithful, and self-controlled, he will be a very good boy. But these virtues in themselves do not qualify him to be a king. As a king-to-be, he must be trained to live and act in a kingly way. The way he sits in a chair or converses with others must be kingly. As one with a dual status—that of a son in the royal family and that of a king-to-be—he must have two kinds of living.

We who believe in Christ Jesus also have a dual status. On the one hand, we are sons of God, members of the divine family. On the other hand, we are kings-to-be, those destined to be kings. Kingship is related to the Israel of God. We should be not only sons of God, but also the Israel of God. To be proper sons of God it is sufficient to have the fruit of the Spirit, such as those virtues listed in 5:22 and 23. But to be kings, the Israel of God, we need another kind of living, a particular kind of walk by the Spirit. We need both the living of sons of God and that of the Israel of God.

Many Christians do not have the first kind of walk by the Spirit, much less the second. We thank the Lord that, by His mercy, many in the church life today do have the first kind of walk by the Spirit to live Christ. But now the Lord is calling us to go on to have the second walk by the Spirit, the second kind of living. This is the living not merely of sons in the divine family, but of those who will be kings in God's kingdom. May our eyes be opened to see that we are kings in the royal family! Our destiny is not only to be sons of God; it is to be kings reigning in the kingdom of God. (*Life-study of Galatians*, pp. 382-383)

Further Reading: Life-study of Galatians, msgs. 30, 43

Enlightenment and inspiration: _____

_____

_____

_____

Morning Nourishment

Rom. ...Those who receive the abundance of grace and of
5:17 the gift of righteousness will reign in life through the
One, Jesus Christ.
21 In order that just as sin reigned in death, so also
grace might reign through righteousness unto eternal life through Jesus Christ our Lord.
Matt. You then pray in this way: Our Father who is in the
6:9-10 heavens, Your name be sanctified; Your kingdom
come; Your will be done, as in heaven, so also on earth.

Do you live in a kingly way? If you live in this way, you will be
kingly even when you laugh. If we see that Paul's word about the
Israel of God implies that we need a kingly walk, the aspiration to
live in a kingly way will be stirred up within us. We may even
want to pray, "Lord, cause me to live and walk in a kingly way so
that I may be qualified to be part of today's Israel of God."
(*Life-study of Galatians,* p. 383)

Today's Reading

In a sense, the nation of Israel is the Israel of God and a testimony of God, even though many Israelites are rebellious and very
sinful. However, the real Israel, the spiritual Israel, is the church.
But because both the nation of Israel and the church are in a low
condition, there is the need for the Lord to recover the real Israel
of God. For such a recovery, we need two kinds of living, two kinds
of walk. In the first walk we shall have such virtues as love, joy,
peace, meekness, and longsuffering, all of which are the expression of the Christ who lives in us. We also need the second kind of
walk so that we may be the Israel of God bearing God's kingship,
representing Him with His authority, and executing His govern-
mental administration.

These two kinds of walks are illustrated by our life as citizens
of the United States. On the one hand, we are persons living in an
ordinary way; on the other hand, we are citizens of this nation. As
persons, we need to be loving, peaceful, joyful, faithful, and meek.
However, in order for the United States to remain a strong nation,

we also need to live as good citizens, fulfilling all the requirements of the government As citizens, we need to pay taxes, serve in the army, and fulfill other obligations. Spiritually speaking, we are both the sons of God and the Israel of God. As sons of God, we need to be loving, joyful, peaceful, faithful, and meek. As the Israel of God, we must walk according to the elementary rules of God's New Testament economy.

Whereas those Christians who truly desire to go on with the Lord usually care only for the first kind of walk and desire to be spiritual, holy, and victorious, we need to care also for the second kind of walk. In particular, we need to care for the church life. However, many Christians who are "spiritual" or "holy" do not care in the least for the church life. These Christians are interested in prayer, Bible study, gospel preaching, or improving their behavior. According to their concept, this is all that is necessary. But because they do not walk according to the principle of the new creation, it is not possible for them to become the Israel of God.

To walk according to the basic principle of the new creation is to walk in a regulated way like soldiers marching in cadence. It is this kind of walk which causes the churches to have impact. The reason the so-called church is weak is that the believers do not have the second kind of walk by the Spirit. They have no real concern for the practice of the church life. But if in a locality there are even a small number of saints who have the second walk and march together in cadence, the church there will have impact. Those saints will not simply be sons of God; they will truly become the Israel of God.

Who defeated the Canaanite tribes, took possession of the good land for the building up of the temple, and brought God's kingdom to earth? It was the Israel of God. Israel in the Old Testament is a type of the church in the New Testament. Thus, the church today must be the Israel of God in reality. Praise the Lord that in God's New Testament economy we have been made both the sons of God and the Israel of God! (*Life-study of Galatians,* pp. 383-386)

Further Reading: Life-study of Galatians, msgs. 30, 43

__Enlightenment and inspiration:__ _____

_____

_____

_____

Morning Nourishment

Gen. And God blessed them; and God said to them, Be
1:28 fruitful and multiply, and fill the earth and subdue it,
      and have dominion...

2:15 And Jehovah God took the man and put him in the
      garden of Eden to work it and to keep it.

Luke Behold, I have given you the authority to tread upon
10:19 serpents and scorpions and over all the power of the
      enemy, and nothing shall by any means hurt you.

Rev. And they overcame him because of the blood of the
12:11 Lamb and because of the word of their testimony,
      and they loved not their soul-life even unto death.

Two words in Genesis are very meaningful. One is "subdue" in Genesis 1:28, which can also be translated "conquer." The other is "keep" in Genesis 2:15, which can also be translated "guard." We see from these verses that God ordained man to conquer and guard the earth. God's original intention was to give the earth to man as a place to dwell. It was not His intention that the earth would become waste (Isa. 45:18). God desired, through man, to not allow Satan to intrude upon the earth, but the problem was that Satan was on earth and intended to do a work of destruction upon it. Therefore, God wanted man to restore the earth from Satan's hand.

Why doesn't God Himself cast Satan into the bottomless pit or the lake of fire?...God can do it, but He does not want to do it Himself. We do not know why He will not do it Himself, but we do know how He is going to do it. God wants to use man to deal with His enemy, and He created man for this purpose. God wants the creature to deal with the creature. He wants His creature *man* to deal with His fallen creature *Satan* in order to bring the earth back to God. The man whom He created is being used by Him for this purpose. (Watchman Nee, *The Glorious Church*, pp. 9-10)

Today's Reading

We must distinguish the difference between the work of saving souls and the work of God. Many times the work of saving souls is not necessarily the work of God. Saving souls solves the problem of man, but the work of God requires that man exercise authority to have dominion over all things created by Him. God needs an authority in His creation, and He has chosen man to be that authority....When God created man,...He revealed His need to have man rule and reign over all His creation and proclaim His triumph. Ruling for God is not a small thing; it is a great matter. God needs men whom He can trust and who will not fail Him. This is God's work, and this is what God desires to obtain.

We do not lightly esteem the work of gospel preaching, but if all our work is just preaching the gospel and saving souls, we are not causing Satan to suffer fatal loss. If man has not restored the earth from the hand of Satan, he has not yet achieved God's purpose in creating him....Saving souls solves man's need, but dealing with Satan satisfies God's need.

Brothers and sisters, this requires us to pay a price. We know how the demons can speak...(Acts 19:15). When a demon meets us, will he flee or not? Preaching the gospel demands that we pay a price, but a much greater price must be paid to deal with Satan.

This is not a matter of a message or a teaching. This requires our practice, and the price is extremely great. If we are to be men whom God will use to overthrow all of Satan's work and authority, we must obey the Lord completely and absolutely! In doing other work it matters less if we preserve ourselves a little, but when dealing with Satan, we cannot leave one bit of ground for ourselves. We may hold on to something of ourselves in our study of the Scriptures, in preaching the gospel, in helping the church or the brothers, but when we are dealing with Satan, self must be utterly abandoned. Satan will never be moved by us if self is preserved. May God open our eyes to see that His purpose demands that we be wholly and absolutely for Him. A double-minded person can never deal with Satan. May God speak this word to our hearts. (Watchman Nee, *The Glorious Church*, pp. 10-12)

Further Reading: The Glorious Church, ch. 1

Enlightenment and inspiration: _____

_____

_____

_____

Morning Nourishment

Exo. And God also said to Moses, Thus you shall say to the
3:15 children of Israel, Jehovah, the God of your fathers,
the God of Abraham, the God of Isaac, and the God of
Jacob, has sent me to you. This is My name forever, and
this is My memorial from generation to generation.

Gen. And he believed Jehovah, and He accounted it to him
15:6 as righteousness.

25:5 And Abraham gave all that he had to Isaac.

49:28 All these are the twelve tribes of Israel, and this is what
their father spoke to them when he blessed them; he
blessed them, each one according to his blessing.

The Bible shows us that God's people had two beginnings. The
first beginning was with Abraham because God's selection and
calling began with Abraham. The other beginning was with the
nation of Israel. God told the Israelites that they would be a people
to Him among all the nations. They would be a kingdom of priests
and a holy nation (Exo. 19:5-6). Hence, Abraham was a definite beginning for God's people, and the nation of Israel was also a definite
beginning for God's people. In between these two beginnings, God
gained three persons, Abraham, Isaac, and Jacob. First there was
Abraham, then there was Isaac, then Jacob, and then the nation of
Israel. From that point on, the nation of Israel became the people of
God, and God had a people of His own. Hence, we can say that
Abraham, Isaac, and Jacob are the foundations of the nation of Israel. Without Abraham, Isaac, and Jacob, there would not be the
nation of Israel, and without Abraham, Isaac, and Jacob, there
would not be a people of God. God's people became His people
through the experience of Abraham, Isaac, and Jacob. (Watchman
Nee, *The God of Abraham, Isaac, and Jacob*, pp. 5-6)

Today's Reading

The book of Genesis reveals the complete Triune God of the
three sections of the life of a corporate person. Genesis does not
consider Abraham, Isaac, and Jacob as three separate persons
but as one complete corporate person with three sections.

In the section of Abraham, we see God the Father who calls man, justifies man, and equips man to live by faith and live in fellowship with Him (Gen. 12:1; 15:6; ch. 17; ch. 18; 19:29; 21:1-13; 22:1-18). Genesis 12:1 shows us the Father's calling and 15:6 reveals His justification. Chapter seventeen shows us how God equipped Abraham to live a life by faith. Then chapter eighteen reveals how God made Abraham to live a life in fellowship with Him.

The section of Isaac represents God the Son, the second of the Triune God, who blesses man with the inheritance of all His riches, with a life of the enjoyment of His abundance, and with a life in peace (Gen. 25:5; 26:3-4, 12-33).

In the life of Jacob with Joseph, we see that the Spirit transforms man and makes man mature in the divine life that man may be able to bless all the people, to rule over all the earth, and to satisfy all the people with God the Son as the life supply (Gen. 27:41; 28:1—35:10; chs. 37, 39—49; Rom. 8:28-29)....The life of Joseph was the completion of the life of his father....Jacob with Joseph blessed all the people, ruled over all the earth, and supplied the whole earth with food. This is in typology. In actuality this refers to God in Christ. God in Christ is the food supply to all the earth. Joseph distributed this food supply, but Joseph was the reality of his father. Thus, Jacob did this with Joseph. The end of Jacob's life with Joseph shows us the maturity in the divine life through the working of God the Spirit.

In the lives of Abraham, Isaac, and Jacob as a corporate person, we can see someone who was loved, chosen, called, and justified by God and made to enjoy all the riches of Christ. Also this one was destined to live a struggling life, a suffering life. Lastly, through all these sufferings this one was transformed by the Spirit and matured in the divine life. When he was old, he knew only to bless people, to reign for God, and to distribute God as the life supply. (*The History of God in His Union with Man,* pp. 135-138)

Further Reading: The History of God in His Union with Man, ch. 10; *The God of Abraham, Isaac, and Jacob,* ch. 1

Enlightenment and inspiration: _____

_____

_____

_____

Morning Nourishment

Gal. But I say, Walk by the Spirit and you shall by no
5:16 means fulfill the lust of the flesh.
  25 If we live by the Spirit, let us also walk by the Spirit.
Col. And have put on the new man, which is being re-
3:10-11 newed unto full knowledge according to the image
     of Him who created him, where...Christ is all and
     in all.

As God's sons, we need a walk by the Spirit to express Christ in
all His virtues. We also need another kind of walk by the Spirit, the
walk according to certain rules or principles, leading toward the
goal for the fulfillment of God's purpose....In order to live a new
creation and live as the Israel of God, we need the second kind of
walk. We need to walk orderly according to the elementary principles of God's economy.

In Galatians 4 we see that we are sons of God with the Spirit of
the Son of God in our hearts. In chapter five we see that we need two
kinds of walk by the Spirit, a general walk to express Christ and a
purposeful walk toward the goal. The second kind of walk constitutes us those who live a new creation and who are the Israel of
God. To live a new creation and to live as the Israel of God, we need
to walk in such a way as to observe all the basic principles of God's
New Testament economy. (*Life-study of Galatians*, pp. 375-376)

Today's Reading

The difference between the old creation and the new creation is
that in the old creation God was not added to man, but in the new
creation He is dispensed into His chosen people. No matter how
good Adam might have been before the fall, God had not been
added to Adam. Adam was good, but he did not have the divine element within him. He was simply the old creation, the creation
without the element of God.

If we as Christians live merely according to the law or according
to ethical standards, we shall live without God. In our living God
will not be mingled with us or saturate us. Even though we may
love others, this love will be in the old creation. But if we are

enlightened, we shall see that as Christians we must walk by the basic principle of the new creation. This basic principle is that God is mingled with us. If we love others according to this principle and not merely according to ethics, God will love in our loving. We shall love others together with God.

The submission a sister renders to her husband may be either of the old creation or of the new creation. On the one hand, in her submission there may be nothing of the mingling with God. Such a submission may simply be according to the standard of a particular culture...[and] is of the old creation. To use the illustration of water and tea, this submission is nothing more than a glass of plain water. It is utterly lacking in the element of tea. How much different is a sister's submission when she lives according to the basic principle of the new creation, the mingling of God with man! Such submission is truly the expression of Christ. It is not simply pure water—it is water mingled with tea. In the case of submission in the old creation, the sister walks according to certain principles or rules assimilated from her culture. But in the case of submission in the new creation, the sister walks according to the basic principle of the new creation. By walking in this way, she lives the new creation. Her walk is not simply according to ethical principles, but according to the principle of the new creation, the principle that man should live by the divine life. Therefore, to live a new creation is to walk by the divine life and divine nature as a governing principle.

What matters today is not whether we are religious or unreligious. What matters is whether or not we are living a new creation. To live a new creation is to live, walk, have our being, and do all things, great and small, with the element of God. In all that we do, we should act not in ourselves, but according to our regenerated being, filled with the divine element. (*Life-study of Galatians,* pp. 377-378, 413-414)

Further Reading: Life-study of Galatians, msgs. 35-40, 46; *The Collected Works of Watchman Nee,* vol. 8, pp. 203-212; *Life-study of Colossians,* msg. 22*

Enlightenment and inspiration: The aspects of the spirit are for life, birth and walk we need to consider the spirit as our aim... this has to do w/ sowing to the spirit sowing a process of the human life day by day we r sowing we sow by what we say and do

Morning Nourishment

Gal. For neither is circumcision anything nor uncircum-
6:15-16 cision, but a new creation *is what matters.* And as
many as walk by this rule, peace be upon them and
mercy, even upon the Israel of God.

Rev. And I saw the holy city, New Jerusalem, coming
21:2 down out of heaven from God, prepared as a bride
adorned for her husband.

According to Galatians 6:15 and 16, the second kind of walk by the Spirit is intimately related to the new creation....The rule [in verse 16] is that of being a new creation [v. 15]. This new creation is equal to the Israel of God, also mentioned in verse 16.

As we have pointed out, the basic principle of the new creation is that a human being lives the divine life. Our daily walk should be regulated by this principle, the principle of living by the divine life. The more we walk according to this principle, the more we shall be the new creation in a practical way. Then others will realize that in our living there is something higher than ethics. They may find it difficult to designate this mysterious element, for it is actually the wonderful person of Christ living in us.

If we live a new creation, we shall be the real Israel of God. According to the book of Genesis, Jacob, a heel-holder, a supplanter, was transformed into Israel, a prince of God and a victor. As a prince and a victor, he could overcome all negative things. Today we need to be such an Israel, a prince to execute God's government on earth. If we have the second kind of walk by the Spirit, an orderly walk according to God's eternal purpose, we shall become a new creation in a very practical way, and we shall also be the Israel of God, representing God, exercising His authority, and carrying out His administration on earth for the fulfillment of His purpose. Ultimately, this Israel of God will become the New Jerusalem. (*Life-study of Galatians,* pp. 376, 379)

Today's Reading

The new Israel of God must be a new creation. For this we need God Himself to be wrought into us, to saturate us, and to make us one with Him. Then we need to live such a mingled life. By living the mingled life of the new creation, we shall be the Israel of God on earth today, His princes and victors executing His authority and representing His government. Today's Israel of God is a miniature of the coming New Jerusalem, which will be the ultimate consummation of the new creation and of the Israel of God. May we all see this and walk according to it!

In Galatians 6:16…Paul does not mention peace in a general way, but in a particular way….This peace is not upon the believers generally; rather, it is upon those who walk by this rule, the elementary rule of the new creation. Peace will be upon those who walk by the rule of the new creation. This indicates that here in the conclusion of Galatians peace is conditional. In order for peace to be upon us, we need to be those who walk by the rule of the new creation to be the true Israel of God.

Before Paul speaks of grace in verse 18, he inserts verse 17 and says, "Henceforth let no one trouble me, for I bear in my body the brands of Jesus." The insertion of this verse is a further indication that at the end of Galatians both peace and grace are mentioned with certain conditions. If peace is to come upon us, we must fulfill the conditions. Because peace here comes upon us in a very particular way, we need to meet a certain requirement, the requirement that we walk by the rule of the new creation to be the Israel of God.

We have pointed out that in Galatians Paul speaks of two kinds of walk by the Spirit. The walk in 5:16 is a more general walk, whereas the walk in 5:25 and 6:16 is a particular walk, a walk according to a certain rule or principle. Having the second kind of walk is a condition for peace to come upon the Israel of God. This is not the peace which comes upon God's people in a general way; it is a specific peace which comes upon a particular people, those who have the second kind of walk by the Spirit. (*Life-study of Galatians,* pp. 379-382)

Further Reading: Life-study of Galatians, msgs. 42-43

Enlightenment and inspiration: The rule of the new creation is walk in the Spirit

Hymns, #947

1   God's Kingdom today is a real exercise,
But when Christ comes to reign it will be a great
     prize;
It is wisdom divine that we now may be trained
That His plan be fulfilled and His justice main-
     tained.

2   God's children, we're born to be kings with His Son,
And we need to be trained that we may overcome
And to know how to rule in His kingdom as kings,
That His kingship thru us be expressed o'er all
     things.

3   Today we must learn to submit to His throne,
How to have a strict life and His government own;
His authority then we'll be able to share,
O'er the nations to rule with God's Son as the heir.

4   With a life strict to self we must righteousness hold,
Kind to others in peace, and with God joyful, bold;
In the Kingdom's reality e'er to remain,
For its manifestation prepared thus to reign.

5   Then Christ when He comes with the kingdom from
     God
Will to us grant His kingship to share as reward;
Thus the Lord will His righteousness thru us main-
     tain
And His wisdom to heavenly powers make plain.

6   For this the Apostle pressed on at all cost,
For the Kingdom assured that he would not be lost;
'Tis for this he charged others, Be true to the Lord,
That the Kingdom might be unto them a reward.

7   O Lord, give us grace for Thy Kingdom to live,
To be trained that Thou may the reward to us give;
Make the Kingdom's reality our exercise,
That its manifestation may be our great prize.

Composition for prophecy with main point and
sub-points: sown into the spirit for the new creation

The Natural life is so
Strong

*The Unique Goal of the Christian Work—
the New Jerusalem*

Scripture Reading: Rev. 21:2, 10, 18-21; 22:1-2; 1 Cor. 3:9,
11-12, 15

Day 1 I. **According to the entire revelation of the
New Testament, the unique goal of the
Christian work should be the New Jerusalem, which is the ultimate goal of God's eternal economy (Rev. 21:2, 10):**

A. The Triune God who passed through all the pro-
cesses, the all-inclusive Christ who was incar-
nated to die and resurrect, and the life-giving
Spirit who was consummated to indwell us all
take the New Jerusalem as Their eternal goal.

B. The Father as the fountain, the Son as the
spring, and the Spirit as the flowing river all
take the New Jerusalem as Their eternal goal
(John 4:14b).

Day 2 C. The degradation of the church is mainly due to
the fact that nearly all the Christian workers
are distracted to take many things other than
the New Jerusalem as their goal.

D. Hence, under the degradation of the church, to
be overcomers answering the Lord's call we
need to overcome not only the negative things
but even more the positive things which replace
the New Jerusalem as the goal.

E. An overcomer's goal should be uniquely and ultimately the goal of God's eternal economy, that is,
the New Jerusalem (Rev. 2:7; 3:12).

Day 3 II. **The New Jerusalem is the Triune God, the
Divine Trinity, as three basic factors,
wrought into and structured together with
His redeemed to be a miraculous structure
of treasure as the conclusion of the whole
Bible:**

A. The first main aspect of the New Jerusalem

is seen in its structure with its base signified
by the gold as the Father's nature, its gates
signified by the pearls as the issue of the Son's
redeeming death and life-dispensing resurrection, and its wall signified by the precious
stones as the consummation of the Spirit's
transforming work (21:12-13, 18-21).

B. The second main aspect of the New Jerusalem is
seen in its furnishings with the reigning center
of the Father signified by the throne, the abiding
place of the Son signified by the temple, and the
enlightening and shining light of the Spirit signified by the oil in the lamp (22:1; 21:16, 22-25;
22:3, 5).

C. The third main aspect of the New Jerusalem is
seen in its supply being the flow of the Divine
Trinity; its base and source for the flow is the
Father signified by the street, its flow is the
Spirit signified by the river of water of life, and
the element of its flow is the Son signified by the
tree of life (vv. 1-2).

D. Thus, the entire constitution of the New Jerusalem is the processed and consummated Triune
God built with His regenerated, transformed,
and glorified elect in His Divine Trinity in a
Day 4   threefold way (cf. Eph. 4:4-6).

III. **As co-workers and elders, we must have the
realization that we are working with God to
carry out His divine building in three aspects—the church, the Body of Christ, and
the New Jerusalem (1 Cor. 3:9, 12a, 15):**

A. We must establish and shepherd the churches
by the pneumatic Christ, the Christ who is the
life-giving Spirit, with His organic salvation.

B. We must build and constitute the Body of Christ
by Christ as the sevenfold intensified Spirit with
His sevenfold intensified organic salvation.

C. We must adorn and consummate the New Jerusalem with God the Father as its golden base,

God the Son as its pearl gates, and God the
Spirit for the wall of precious stones, by drinking the Spirit, the flowing Triune God, as the
river of water of life and eating Christ, the overcoming Lion-Lamb, as the tree of life with His
rich and fresh supply:

1. The New Jerusalem needs not only to be
   consummated but also adorned; she is "prepared as a bride adorned for her husband"
   Day 5 (Rev. 21:2, 18-21).
2. We need to adorn the divine building by
   coordinating with the transforming Spirit
   to minister the Triune God into others, perfecting them with the attributes of the
   Triune God so that these divine attributes
   become their human virtues for the building up of the Body of Christ (2 Cor. 3:18;
   S. S. 1:10-11; Eph. 4:11-12).

D. Even today the New Jerusalem is still under
   construction; we are building up the Body of
   Christ for the building of the New Jerusalem:

1. We are working together with God to build
   up the New Jerusalem; the Lord's concern
   is to gain the New Jerusalem through the
   precursor of the organic Body of Christ produced in the churches.
2. As we grow in the divine life and minister
   the Triune God to others for their growth in
   the divine life, we are building up the Body
   of Christ to consummate the New Jerusa-
   Day 6 lem (Col. 2:19; Eph. 4:16).

IV. **What is crucial with our building work is "of
    what sort it is" (1 Cor. 3:13):**

A. If we build upon the foundation with gold (God
   the Father in His divine nature), silver (God the
   Son in His judicial redemption), and precious
   stones (God the Spirit in His transforming
   work), we will receive a reward (v. 12a, 14).

B. If we build upon the foundation with wood (the

human nature), grass (man in the flesh), and stubble (lifelessness), we will suffer loss; our work will be consumed, but we ourselves will be saved, yet so as through fire (v. 12b, 15).

V. "In the past there was a large frame in my study in which these words were written: '...he himself will be saved, yet so as through fire' (1 Cor. 3:15). If you build the temple of God with gold, silver, and precious stones, you will receive a reward. However, if you build with wood, grass, and stubble, your work will be consumed, but you yourself will be saved, yet so as through fire. This may be likened to a piece of land that was on fire, and the wood, grass, and stubble upon it were burned. The land itself could not be consumed, yet it went through the burning by fire. I hung that portion of 1 Corinthians on the wall in my home so that I might always be reminded: 'Man, be careful; do not try to build the Body of Christ and the New Jerusalem with your nature, disposition, old "I," old creation, self, inclination, and preference. If you do, you will destroy the Body of Christ.' Whenever we touch the eternal goal of God, the New Jerusalem, we need to be very pure; we must not be careless" (*How to Be a Co-worker and an Elder and How to Fulfill Their Obligations*, pp. 89-90).

Morning Nourishment

Rev. **And he carried me away in spirit onto a great and**
21:10 **high mountain and showed me the holy city, Jeru-**
salem, coming down out of heaven from God.
John **...The water that I will give him will become in him**
4:14 **a fountain of water springing up into eternal life.**

The accepting of the divine revelation must also be governed
by the Body of Christ which consummates the New Jerusalem
as the divine goal of the processed and consummated Triune
God. John 4:14 says, "The water that I will give him will become
in him a fountain of water springing up into eternal life." The
Triune God is a fountain emerging to be a spring and gushing up
to be a river flowing into eternal life. The fountain is God the Father, the spring is God the Son, and the river is God the Spirit
flowing as living water into eternal life. For more than fifty years
I tried to understand the phrase "into eternal life," but I was unable. In recent days, however, I have come to know the meaning.
Into eternal life does not mean to enter into eternal life. It means
to become the eternal life. The flowing of the Father as the fountain, the Son as the spring, and the Spirit as the river eventually
becomes the eternal life, which is the New Jerusalem. The entire
Bible shows us that our God is the flowing God. God flowed in
the Father as the fountain, and the Father emerged, was manifested, to be the Son as the spring, and the gushing river is the
Spirit. The issue, the consummation, of this flowing is the New
Jerusalem. From Genesis to Revelation the entire Bible speaks
only about this flowing Triune God, and the issue of Their flowing is the New Jerusalem. Just as a man is the consummation of
the human life, the consummation of the divine life is the New
Jerusalem. (*A Word of Love to the Co-workers, Elders, Lovers,
and Seekers of the Lord,* p. 62)

Today's Reading

In [the] crystallization-study [of the Gospel of John] I thoroughly and intrinsically came to the clear conclusion that this
Gospel, especially from chapter one to chapter four, is the record

of the flowing God in His three stages: the Father as the fountain, the Son as the spring, and the Spirit as the flowing river. Moreover, They all take the New Jerusalem as Their eternal goal. Apparently, the New Jerusalem is not mentioned in John. However, it is seen in the eternal life in 4:14. Eternal life here is the totality of the divine life. A man is the totality of the human life; each one of us is the totality of the human life, but the divine life has only one totality in the whole universe—the New Jerusalem.

The Bible teaches us that eternal life is God Himself. In the beginning there is God as the eternal life, and the consummation of God as the eternal life is the New Jerusalem. The Bible consummates in the New Jerusalem, which is the very God who was in the beginning. How does God become the New Jerusalem? It is through His flowing. The Bible has two ends, Genesis 1—2 and Revelation 21—22. At the beginning of the Bible there is God, at the end there is the New Jerusalem, and in between are hundreds of pages speaking about all the matters related to the eternal life, including the believers, regeneration, transformation, conformation, and glorification. This is the proper way to view the Bible. All the activities of the eternal life take the New Jerusalem as the final goal. This is the meaning of "into eternal life" in John 4:14. The word into is also used in 1 Corinthians 12:13, which says that the Gentiles and the Jews have all been baptized in one Spirit into one Body. "Into one Body" does not mean merely to enter into the Body but to become the Body. In the same way, "into eternal life"does not merely mean to enter into the New Jerusalem as the eternal life but to become the New Jerusalem as the eternal life. The coming New Jerusalem will be you and me. We are the New Jerusalem. The New Jerusalem is still under a consummating work, and this consummating work is the flow of the divine life. This is very deep. (*A Word of Love to the Co-workers, Elders, Lovers, and Seekers of the Lord,* pp. 23-24)

Further Reading: A Word of Love to the Co-workers, Elders, Lovers, and Seekers of the Lord, chs. 2, 4

Enlightenment and inspiration: _____

_____

_____

_____

Morning Nourishment

Rev. ...To him who overcomes, to him I will give to eat of
2:7 the tree of life, which is in the Paradise of God.
3:12 He who overcomes, him I will make a pillar in the
temple of My God, and he shall by no means go out
anymore, and I will write upon him the name of
My God and the name of the city of My God, the New
Jerusalem, which descends out of heaven from My
God, and My new name.

According to the entire revelation of the New Testament,
the unique goal of the Christian work should be the New Jerusalem, which is the ultimate goal of God's eternal economy.

In the Lord's recovery, what is our goal? Is it to be people
who are holy? Today among Christians in general, nearly no
one has a proper goal. They pursue being spiritual, being holy,
preaching the gospel to win souls, and establishing seminaries
to teach theology and the Bible, yet hardly anyone can say that
they are doing these things with the goal of consummating the
New Jerusalem. They have all missed the proper goal. (*How to
Be a Co-worker and an Elder and How to Fulfill Their Obligations,* p. 49)

Today's Reading

God has only one ultimate goal, that is, the New Jerusalem.
This is a very clear and definite matter in the Bible. The Bible
with its sixty-six books opens with "In the beginning God...." In
the beginning of the Bible there was God only and nothing
else.... At the end of the Bible, however, we reach the New Jerusalem. Between the beginning and the end, there is a course of
much history with many ages...in which many things take
place and in which God does a great deal of work. However,
regardless of how many ages there are and how much work
God does, He has only one goal. In the beginning of the Bible
there is one single God, and at the end there is a great, corporate God—the New Jerusalem.

Today, the majority of Christians disregard the New

Jerusalem, the tree of life, and the river of water of life. Instead, they take many other good things as replacements of the New Jerusalem. But the Lord's recovery is not like that. Today we establish the churches, edify the saints, practice the vital groups, and visit people by door-knocking, but our aim, our goal, is for the consummation of the New Jerusalem.

The degradation of the church is mainly due to the fact that nearly all Christian workers have been distracted to take many things other than the New Jerusalem as their goal. Hence, under the degradation of the church, to be overcomers answering the Lord's call, we need to overcome not only the negative things but even more the positive things which replace the New Jerusalem as the goal.

To be overcomers we should take the goal of God's eternal economy, the New Jerusalem, as our unique and ultimate goal. We all need to remember this goal. Our goal is not to help people to be spiritual or to be holy. Rather, we are leading people toward the New Jerusalem to consummate the New Jerusalem. How do we do this? It is by drinking the Spirit and eating Christ for us to receive His rich and fresh supply. Thus, we adorn and consummate the New Jerusalem with God the Father as its golden base, God the Son as its pearl gates, and God the Spirit for its wall of precious stones. It is not according to your will, nor by using your way, nor with you as the element and essence. Rather, it is with God as the essence, Christ as the element, and the Spirit as the way. We need to daily drink the flowing God, the Spirit, as our river of water of life; we need to eat the overcoming Lion-Lamb as the tree of life to be our fresh and rich supply; and we need to take the Triune God as the essence, the element, and the way to build and consummate the New Jerusalem. This is the consummation of the full ministry of Christ. (*How to Be a Co-worker and an Elder and How to Fulfill Their Obligations,* pp. 49-52)

Further Reading: How to Be a Co-worker and an Elder and How to Fulfill Their Obligations, ch. 3

Enlightenment and inspiration: _____
_____
_____
_____

Morning Nourishment

Rev. **And the building work of its wall was jasper; and**
21:18 **the city was pure gold, like clear glass.**
   21 **And the twelve gates were twelve pearls; each one**
      of the gates was, respectively, of one pearl....
22:1-2 **And he showed me a river of water of life, bright as**
      crystal, proceeding out of the throne of God and of
      the Lamb in the middle of its street. And on this side
      and on that side of the river was the tree of life, pro-
      ducing twelve fruits, yielding its fruit each month...

If we look at today's outward situation, we can see the lack of the building up of the Body of Christ which consummates the New Jerusalem. This is why the Lord has charged me to release the high peaks of His divine revelation. First, we need to release the truth that God became a man so that man may become God in life and in nature but not in the Godhead. Then we need to release the truth concerning the New Jerusalem. My burden is to release these two great truths.

The New Jerusalem is constructed with the Triune God as the main factors. It is furnished with the Triune God as the throne, as the temple (the palace), and as the lamp. Also, New Jerusalem is a city supplied by the Triune God—the Father as the source and the base, the Spirit as the flow, the river, and the Son as the main supply to nourish the entire city. Through this nourishment and divine beverage we members of the new city grow in the divine life and are built together. (*The Application of the Interpretation of the New Jerusalem to the Seeking Believers,* pp. 54-56)

Today's Reading

From now on we must consider that our work is a building work by the growth of the saints in the divine life. The divine life is the Divine Trinity, who is the structure, the furnishings, and the supply of the holy city. As we grow in the divine life and minister the Triune God to others for their growth in the divine life, we are building up the Body of Christ, which will consummate the New Jerusalem. We need to experience and speak these things.

The more we speak, the more we will have to speak. The more we speak, the more we will be nourished and satisfied. From now on the co-workers and the elders must know how to speak these things.

The New Jerusalem is an organic constitution of the processed and consummated Triune God with His regenerated, transformed, and glorified elect. It has a threefold stress with the Divine Trinity in the three main aspects of this organic constitution:

1. The first main aspect is its structure with its base signified by the gold as the Father's nature, its gates signified by the pearls as the issue of the Son's redeeming death and life-dispensing resurrection, and its wall signified by the precious stones as the consummation of the Spirit's transforming work.

2. The second main aspect is its furnishings with the reigning center of the Father signified by the throne, the abiding place of the Son signified by the temple, and the enlightening and shining light of the Spirit signified by the oil in the lamp.

3. The third main aspect is its supply being the flow of the Divine Trinity; its base and source for the flow is the Father signified by the street, its flow is the Spirit signified by the river of the water of life, and the element of its flow is the Son signified by the tree of life.

The entire constitution of the New Jerusalem is the processed and consummated Triune God built with His regenerated, transformed, and glorified elect in His Divine Trinity in a threefold way. It is impossible for such a constitution to be anything physical; it has to be the Divine Trinity in His threefold blending with His redeemed elect. May we receive the eternal mercy and the sufficient grace of the unlimited Christ that we could live a life as a foretaste of such an organic constitution in this age for its full taste in eternity. (*The Application of the Interpretation of the New Jerusalem to the Seeking Believers*, pp. 54-56)

Further Reading: The Building Work of God, ch. 4; The Application of the Interpretation of the New Jerusalem to the Seeking Believers, msg. 5

Enlightenment and inspiration: _____

_____
_____
_____

Morning Nourishment

1 Cor. For we are God's fellow workers; you are God's cul-
3:9 tivated land, God's building.

Rev. And I saw the holy city, New Jerusalem, coming
21:2 down out of heaven from God, prepared as a bride
adorned for her husband.

19 The foundations of the wall of the city were
adorned with every precious stone...

The three aspects of God's divine building are the church, the Body of Christ, and the New Jerusalem. To work with God, to carry out the divine building of God in its three aspects, we co-workers and elders must first establish and shepherd the churches by the pneumatic Christ, the Christ who is the life-giving Spirit. We must build up the churches by the pneumatic Christ. The building of the church is the ministry of Christ in His second stage. In His first stage there was only the mentioning of the church (Matt. 16:18; 18:17); there was not yet the actual building of the church. In the first stage He accomplished only the judicial redemption to redeem back the chosen people of God to be the material for the building of the church. The church is not built by Him in the ministry of His incarnation; the building of the church is accomplished by the pneumatic Christ as the Spirit in the ministry of His becoming the Spirit. (*How to Be a Co-worker and an Elder and How to Fulfill Their Obligations*, p. 86)

Today's Reading

Our establishing and shepherding the churches should be carried out not only by Christ, who is the life-giving Spirit, but also by our applying His organic salvation.

The second aspect of the divine building is the Body of Christ. We need to build and constitute the Body of Christ by Christ as the sevenfold intensified Spirit with His sevenfold intensified organic salvation. This brings us into the third stage of Christ's full ministry, which is the stage of His intensification. The building of the church was not in the first stage, and strictly speaking, it is also not in the second stage, because it was not carried out successfully. In the second stage God was building the church. However, instead of going forward, the church fell backward and degraded into a defeated church. Hence, in Revelation, Christ has become the sevenfold intensified Spirit to build and constitute the Body of Christ in a sevenfold intensified way.

We must build and constitute the Body of Christ with life....Before we begin the building of the Body of Christ, we must know the church. Therefore, we must begin with the second stage and then enter into the third stage. After we have entered into the third stage, we should not go backward, but we must remain in the third stage to daily experience the sevenfold intensification so that we may build and constitute the Body of Christ by Christ as the sevenfold intensified Spirit with His sevenfold intensified organic salvation.

The New Jerusalem is the third aspect of the divine building. We need to adorn and consummate the New Jerusalem with God the Father as its golden base, God the Son as its pearl gates, and God the Spirit for its wall of precious stones, by drinking the Spirit, the flowing Triune God, as the river of water of life and eating Christ, the overcoming Lion-Lamb, as the tree of life with His rich and fresh supply....Revelation 21:2 says that the New Jerusalem was "prepared as a bride adorned for her husband." To "adorn" oneself is to make oneself pretty. This term cannot be used for males; it can be applied only to females.

The expressions used in the Holy Scriptures are very precious. You have read Revelation a number of times, but have you ever noticed the word *adorned*? I have read the Bible for many years, but it was not until this time when I was writing the message outlines that I found out that the New Jerusalem needs to be not only consummated but also adorned (Rev. 21:19). It is adorned with pure gold, pearls, and precious stones, that is, with the Triune God as the elements. (*How to Be a Co-worker and an Elder and How to Fulfill Their Obligations,* pp. 86-88)

Further Reading: How to Be a Co-worker and an Elder and How to Fulfill Their Obligations, ch. 6

Enlightenment and inspiration: _____

_____

_____

_____

Morning Nourishment

2 Cor. But we all with unveiled face, beholding and reflect-
3:18 ing like a mirror the glory of the Lord, are being
transformed into the same image from glory to glory,
even as from the Lord Spirit.
S. S. Your cheeks are lovely with plaits of ornaments,
1:10-11 your neck with strings of jewels. We will make you
plaits of gold with studs of silver.

The seeker's transformation in Song of Songs can be seen in
the description of her in 1:10-11....The perfected ones who have
experienced this kind of transformation know how to perfect others. We all need to learn how to perfect others with the attributes
of the Triune God. We need to know what the person before us
needs. We should not look merely at a person's mistakes. Instead,
we should realize that they are short of God's golden nature and
life. They are short of Christ's death, resurrection, and ascension.
They are short of the Holy Spirit's work. We have to add all these
things to them. We should not condemn others; instead, we
should minister the life supply to them. We need to impress them
that in the proper church life we pay our attention fully to the Triune God: God the Father as the divine nature and life, God the
Son as the divine element, and God the Spirit as the transforming
One in His divine essence. This is to minister the Triune God to
them. (*Crystallization-study of Song of Songs*, pp. 35-36)

Today's Reading

Transformation in the church life is carried out by the transforming Spirit. Second Corinthians 3:18 says that we are transformed by the Lord Spirit. Ultimately, the Spirit, the third of the
Divine Trinity, has been processed, consummated, and com-
pounded into the transforming all-inclusive Spirit, who is the consummated Triune God. The consummated Triune God is the
transforming One.

In this transforming work there is the need of the Triune God
to be the transforming Spirit, and there is the need of the coordination of some "transformers." In Ephesians 4 these transformers

are referred to as perfecters. Ephesians 4:11-12 says that God has given some apostles, prophets, evangelists, and shepherds and teachers to perfect the saints to do the work of the ministry, that is, to build up the Body of Christ. Where are the perfecters today who know how to cooperate with the transforming Triune God?

To have plaited hair is an indication of submission to the Head, to the throne....The lover of Christ has been transformed by the transforming Triune God to have plaited hair. Then the co-ordinators, the perfecting ones, say, "We will make you plaits of gold" (S. S. 1:11). Notice the word *we*, which refers to the perfecters. This means that the perfecters coordinate with the perfecting Spirit to put gold into the seeker's plaits. Gold refers to God the Father in His divine nature. Our submission to God's headship under His throne must be according to the divine nature.

The plaits of gold are fastened with studs of silver. The silver studs are the fasteners and refer to the redeeming Christ. Only the redeeming Christ holds us, fastens us, so that we are not scattered. Christ accomplished God's complete redemption, so whatever He has done is altogether legal, judicial.

The element of gold is wrought into the lover's bound hair, and the plaits of gold are fastened by silver studs. Also, the seeker's neck is adorned with strings of jewels (S. S. 1:10). Jewels are precious stones. These precious stones put together as one into strings signify the transforming Spirit.

I have the full assurance that what I am doing here will go to the New Jerusalem. If we want what we do to be in the New Jerusalem, we need to learn how to add gold into the plaits of hair, how to make silver studs to hold the plaits of hair, and how to make strings of jewels, precious stones, to cover the naked neck....We must learn to minister the Triune God in a practical way to others for their transformation. (*Crystallization-study of Song of Songs,* pp. 41-43)

Further Reading: Crystallization-study of Song of Songs, msgs. 3-4; *The God-men,* ch. 4; *The Practical Points concerning Blending,* ch. 4

Enlightenment and inspiration: _____

_____

_____

_____

Morning Nourishment

1 Cor. But if anyone builds upon the foundation gold, 3:12-15 silver, precious stones, wood, grass, stubble, the work of each will become manifest; for the day will declare *it*, because it is revealed by fire, and the fire itself will prove each one's work, of what sort it is. If anyone's work which he has built upon *the foundation* remains, he will receive a reward; if anyone's work is consumed, he will suffer loss, but he himself will be saved, yet so as through fire.

The proper building materials for the church are gold, silver, and precious stones (1 Cor. 3:12a). Gold symbolizes the divine nature of God the Father. Silver symbolizes Christ's redemptive work. Precious stones symbolize the Spirit's transforming work. This indicates that what we build upon the foundation of Christ should be something of the Triune God—the Father, the Son, and the Spirit.

We should not build the church with wood, grass, and stubble (1 Cor. 3:12b). Just as gold signifies God's nature, wood signifies the human nature. Grass signifies man in the flesh (Isa. 40:6-7). Stubble signifies lifelessness. Stubble is the stump of the crops after being reaped. With the stubble there is no seed, no life. We have to admit that most of the work in Christianity is according to and out of these three negative items—the human nature, the human flesh, and lifelessness. (*Basic Lessons on Service*, pp. 122-123)

Today's Reading

We may appreciate certain brothers' capabilities for doing things, but in the church life the main thing is not to accomplish things. The main thing is to build with the Triune God upon the foundation already laid, that is, upon the all-inclusive Christ. If we just depend upon our capability, talent, or skill to finish something, that means we are serving according to wood, grass, and stubble, not gold, silver, and precious stone. We need to serve with the Father's nature, in the Son's redeeming way with the cross, and by the transforming Spirit. If we serve according to ourselves, there is no transformation, no cross, and no divine nature. Then what we do is just a secular thing which has nothing to do with the church. The church is altogether a composition of gold, silver, and precious stone—the Father, the Son, and the Spirit.

The apostle Paul told us in 1 Corinthians 3 that every man's work will be tested by fire (vv. 13-15)....[The reward in verse 14] has nothing to do with salvation. In verses 14 and 15, both reward and salvation are mentioned. The reward is not for salvation. Neither can salvation replace the reward.

If our work, our service, is really of gold, silver, and precious stone, it can stand the test of fire. These materials will not be burned. If our work is with these materials, we will receive a reward. The reward in the coming age will be the richer and higher enjoyment of the Lord. Today in our church life, in our work, in our service, we enjoy the Lord. But in the coming age the reward will be the richer, higher, and greater enjoyment of Christ. Apparently speaking, that will be an entering into the manifestation of the kingdom of the heavens, but our entering the kingdom is for the greater, higher, and richer enjoyment of Christ.

Verse 15 says, "If anyone's work is consumed, he will suffer loss, but he himself will be saved, yet so as through fire." Wood, grass, and stubble are not good for building materials but good for being burned. Today many Christians are producing fuel for a burning to come. The more they do, the more they have something for burning.

If anyone's work is consumed, he will suffer loss. *Loss* here means that he will lose the reward. He will lose the richer, higher, and greater enjoyment of Christ. The Word says clearly...that he himself will be saved, yet he will be saved as through fire. This indicates some kind of punishment and discipline, not just a loss.

We saw in the previous lesson that we must avoid anything of strange fire in our service. Also, all the work of wood, grass, and stubble must be avoided. We must build with gold, silver, and precious stone. (*Basic Lessons on Service,* pp. 123-124)

Further Reading: Basic Lessons on Service, lsn. 15

Enlightenment and inspiration: _____
_____
_____
_____

Hymns, #975

1 It was a garden in the primal age,
   But at the end it is a city square;
   Creation's center in the garden was,
   God's building issues in the city fair.

2 Both in the garden and the city fair
   A river and the tree of life are seen,
   Christ typifying as the life supply,
   The Spirit showing as the living stream.

3 Both in the garden and the city bright
   Three kinds of precious substances are found;
   There are the gold, the pearls, and precious stones
   Which for the building work of God abound.

4 But in the garden all these precious things
   Are just materials lying in the earth,
   Yet in the city all are builded up
   And form that dwelling of transcendent worth.

5 Man in the garden of the clay was formed,
   In nature as the Lord created him;
   The tree of life was then without the man,
   Not having yet become his life within.

6 But in the city glorious the tree
   Within the corporate "man" doth grow, thereby
   Revealing Christ Himself as life divine
   Being to man his inward life supply.

7 'Tis for the city man is wrought upon,
   Therefore regenerated and transformed
   To purest gold, to pearls and precious stones,
   As Christ's own Body, to Himself conformed.

8 Within the garden also was a bride,
   Who was to Adam as his counterpart;
   Lastly, the city is itself the bride
   As Christ's own fulness, precious to His heart.

9 The city is God's building work replete,
   A composition of the justified;
   A habitation it affords to God
   And is to Christ His own beloved bride.

10 'Tis God's expression, ultimate and full,
     Corporate and universal, marvelous;
     God's glory it completely manifests,
     And is Christ's counterpart most glorious.

Composition for prophecy with main point and sub-points: Turn to your spirit!

touch the pul coming one.

Get rid of the wood, hay and stubble

BFA Mailing (mo)

Europe

Reading Schedule for the Recovery Version of the New Testament with Footnotes

Wk.	Lord's Day	Monday	Tuesday	Wednesday	Thursday	Friday	Saturday
1	Matt 1:1-2	1:3-7	1:8-17	1:18-25	2:1-23	3:1-6	3:7-17
2	4:1-11	4:12-25	5:1-4	5:5-12	5:13-20	5:21-26	5:27-48
3	6:1-8	6:9-18	6:19-34	7:1-12	7:13-29	8:1-13	8:14-22
4	8:23-34	9:1-13	9:14-17	9:18-34	9:35—10:5	10:6-25	10:26-42
5	11:1-15	11:16-30	12:1-14	12:15-32	12:33-42	12:43—13:2	13:3-12
6	13:13-30	13:31-43	13:44-58	14:1-13	14:14-21	14:22-36	15:1-20
7	15:21-31	15:32-39	16:1-12	16:13-20	16:21-28	17:1-13	17:14-27
8	18:1-14	18:15-22	18:23-35	19:1-15	19:16-30	20:1-16	20:17-34
9	21:1-11	21:12-22	21:23-32	21:33-46	22:1-22	22:23-33	22:34-46
10	23:1-12	23:13-39	24:1-14	24:15-31	24:32-51	25:1-13	25:14-30
11	25:31-46	26:1-16	26:17-35	26:36-46	26:47-64	26:65-75	27:1-26
12	27:27-44	27:45-56	27:57—28:15	28:16-20	Mark 1:1	1:2-6	1:7-13
13	1:14-28	1:29-45	2:1-12	2:13-28	3:1-19	3:20-35	4:1-25
14	4:26-41	5:1-20	5:21-43	6:1-29	6:30-56	7:1-23	7:24-37
15	8:1-26	8:27—9:1	9:2-29	9:30-50	10:1-16	10:17-34	10:35-52
16	11:1-16	11:17-33	12:1-27	12:28-44	13:1-13	13:14-37	14:1-26
17	14:27-52	14:53-72	15:1-15	15:16-47	16:1-8	16:9-20	Luke 1:1-4
18	1:5-25	1:26-46	1:47-56	1:57-80	2:1-8	2:9-20	2:21-39
19	2:40-52	3:1-20	3:21-38	4:1-13	4:14-30	4:31-44	5:1-26
20	5:27—6:16	6:17-38	6:39-49	7:1-17	7:18-23	7:24-35	7:36-50
21	8:1-15	8:16-25	8:26-39	8:40-56	9:1-17	9:18-26	9:27-36
22	9:37-50	9:51-62	10:1-11	10:12-24	10:25-37	10:38-42	11:1-13
23	11:14-26	11:27-36	11:37-54	12:1-12	12:13-21	12:22-34	12:35-48
24	12:49-59	13:1-9	13:10-17	13:18-30	13:31—14:6	14:7-14	14:15-24
25	14:25-35	15:1-10	15:11-21	15:22-32	16:1-13	16:14-22	16:23-31
26	17:1-19	17:20-37	18:1-14	18:15-30	18:31-43	19:1-10	19:11-27

Reading Schedule for the Recovery Version of the New Testament with Footnotes

Wk.	Lord's Day	Monday	Tuesday	Wednesday	Thursday	Friday	Saturday
27	☐ Luke 19:28-48	☐ 20:1-19	☐ 20:20-38	☐ 20:39—21:4	☐ 21:5-27	☐ 21:28-38	☐ 22:1-20
28	☐ 22:21-38	☐ 22:39-54	☐ 22:55-71	☐ 23:1-43	☐ 23:44-56	☐ 24:1-12	☐ 24:13-35
29	☐ 24:36-53	☐ John 1:1-13	☐ 1:14-18	☐ 1:19-34	☐ 1:35-51	☐ 2:1-11	☐ 2:12-22
30	☐ 2:23—3:13	☐ 3:14-21	☐ 3:22-36	☐ 4:1-14	☐ 4:15-26	☐ 4:27-42	☐ 4:43-54
31	☐ 5:1-16	☐ 5:17-30	☐ 5:31-47	☐ 6:1-15	☐ 6:16-31	☐ 6:32-51	☐ 6:52-71
32	☐ 7:1-9	☐ 7:10-24	☐ 7:25-36	☐ 7:37-52	☐ 7:53—8:11	☐ 8:12-27	☐ 8:28-44
33	☐ 8:45-59	☐ 9:1-13	☐ 9:14-34	☐ 9:35—10:9	☐ 10:10-30	☐ 10:31—11:4	☐ 11:5-22
34	☐ 11:23-40	☐ 11:41-57	☐ 12:1-11	☐ 12:12-24	☐ 12:25-36	☐ 12:37-50	☐ 13:1-11
35	☐ 13:12-30	☐ 13:31-38	☐ 14:1-6	☐ 14:7-20	☐ 14:21-31	☐ 15:1-11	☐ 15:12-27
36	☐ 16:1-15	☐ 16:16-33	☐ 17:1-5	☐ 17:6-13	☐ 17:14-24	☐ 17:25—18:11	☐ 18:12-27
37	☐ 18:28-40	☐ 19:1-16	☐ 19:17-30	☐ 19:31-42	☐ 20:1-13	☐ 20:14-18	☐ 20:19-22
38	☐ 20:23-31	☐ 21:1-14	☐ 21:15-22	☐ 21:23-25	☐ Acts 1:1-8	☐ 1:9-14	☐ 1:15-26
39	☐ 2:1-13	☐ 2:14-21	☐ 2:22-36	☐ 2:37-41	☐ 2:42-47	☐ 3:1-18	☐ 3:19—4:22
40	☐ 4:23-37	☐ 5:1-16	☐ 5:17-32	☐ 5:33-42	☐ 6:1—7:1	☐ 7:2-29	☐ 7:30-60
41	☐ 8:1-13	☐ 8:14-25	☐ 8:26-40	☐ 9:1-19	☐ 9:20-43	☐ 10:1-16	☐ 10:17-33
42	☐ 10:34-48	☐ 11:1-18	☐ 11:19-30	☐ 12:1-25	☐ 13:1-12	☐ 13:13-43	☐ 13:44—14:5
43	☐ 14:6-28	☐ 15:1-12	☐ 15:13-34	☐ 15:35—16:5	☐ 16:6-18	☐ 16:19-40	☐ 17:1-18
44	☐ 17:19-34	☐ 18:1-17	☐ 18:18-28	☐ 19:1-20	☐ 19:21-41	☐ 20:1-12	☐ 20:13-38
45	☐ 21:1-14	☐ 21:15-26	☐ 21:27-40	☐ 22:1-21	☐ 22:22-29	☐ 22:30—23:11	☐ 23:12-15
46	☐ 23:16-30	☐ 23:31—24:21	☐ 24:22—25:5	☐ 25:6-27	☐ 26:1-13	☐ 26:14-32	☐ 27:1-26
47	☐ 27:27—28:10	☐ 28:11-22	☐ 28:23-31	☐ Rom 1:1-2	☐ 1:3-7	☐ 1:8-17	☐ 1:18-25
48	☐ 1:26—2:10	☐ 2:11-29	☐ 3:1-20	☐ 3:21-31	☐ 4:1-12	☐ 4:13-25	☐ 5:1-11
49	☐ 5:12-17	☐ 5:18—6:5	☐ 6:6-11	☐ 6:12-23	☐ 7:1-12	☐ 7:13-25	☐ 8:1-2
50	☐ 8:3-6	☐ 8:7-13	☐ 8:14-25	☐ 8:26-39	☐ 9:1-18	☐ 9:19—10:3	☐ 10:4-15
51	☐ 10:16—11:10	☐ 11:11-22	☐ 11:23-36	☐ 12:1-3	☐ 12:4-21	☐ 13:1-14	☐ 14:1-12
52	☐ 14:13-23	☐ 15:1-13	☐ 15:14-33	☐ 16:1-5	☐ 16:6-24	☐ 16:25-27	☐ I Cor 1:1-4

Reading Schedule for the Recovery Version of the New Testament with Footnotes

Wk.	Lord's Day	Monday	Tuesday	Wednesday	Thursday	Friday	Saturday
53	☐ I Cor 1:5-9	☐ 1:10-17	☐ 1:18-31	☐ 2:1-5	☐ 2:6-10	☐ 2:11-16	☐ 3:1-9
54	☐ 3:10-13	☐ 3:14-23	☐ 4:1-9	☐ 4:10-21	☐ 5:1-13	☐ 6:1-11	☐ 6:12-20
55	☐ 7:1-16	☐ 7:17-24	☐ 7:25-40	☐ 8:1-13	☐ 9:1-15	☐ 9:16-27	☐ 10:1-4
56	☐ 10:5-13	☐ 10:14-33	☐ 11:1-6	☐ 11:7-16	☐ 11:17-26	☐ 11:27-34	☐ 12:1-11
57	☐ 12:12-22	☐ 12:23-31	☐ 13:1-13	☐ 14:1-12	☐ 14:13-25	☐ 14:26-33	☐ 14:34-40
58	☐ 15:1-19	☐ 15:20-28	☐ 15:29-34	☐ 15:35-49	☐ 15:50-58	☐ 16:1-9	☐ 16:10-24
59	☐ II Cor 1:1-4	☐ 1:5-14	☐ 1:15-22	☐ 1:23—2:11	☐ 2:12-17	☐ 3:1-6	☐ 3:7-11
60	☐ 3:12-18	☐ 4:1-6	☐ 4:7-12	☐ 4:13-18	☐ 5:1-8	☐ 5:9-15	☐ 5:16-21
61	☐ 6:1-13	☐ 6:14—7:4	☐ 7:5-16	☐ 8:1-15	☐ 8:16-24	☐ 9:1-15	☐ 10:1-6
62	☐ 10:7-18	☐ 11:1-15	☐ 11:16-33	☐ 12:1-10	☐ 12:11-21	☐ 13:1-10	☐ 13:11-14
63	☐ Gal 1:1-5	☐ 1:6-14	☐ 1:15-24	☐ 2:1-13	☐ 2:14-21	☐ 3:1-4	☐ 3:5-14
64	☐ 3:15-22	☐ 3:23-29	☐ 4:1-7	☐ 4:8-20	☐ 4:21-31	☐ 5:1-12	☐ 5:13-21
65	☐ 5:22-26	☐ 6:1-10	☐ 6:11-15	☐ 6:16-18	☐ Eph 1:1-3	☐ 1:4-6	☐ 1:7-10
66	☐ 1:11-14	☐ 1:15-18	☐ 1:19-23	☐ 2:1-5	☐ 2:6-10	☐ 2:11-14	☐ 2:15-18
67	☐ 2:19-22	☐ 3:1-7	☐ 3:8-13	☐ 3:14-18	☐ 3:19-21	☐ 4:1-4	☐ 4:5-10
68	☐ 4:11-16	☐ 4:17-24	☐ 4:25-32	☐ 5:1-10	☐ 5:11-21	☐ 5:22-26	☐ 5:27-33
69	☐ 6:1-9	☐ 6:10-14	☐ 6:15-18	☐ 6:19-24	☐ Phil 1:1-7	☐ 1:8-18	☐ 1:19-26
70	☐ 1:27—2:4	☐ 2:5-11	☐ 2:12-16	☐ 2:17-30	☐ 3:1-6	☐ 3:7-11	☐ 3:12-16
71	☐ 3:17-21	☐ 4:1-9	☐ 4:10-23	☐ Col 1:1-8	☐ 1:9-13	☐ 1:14-23	☐ 1:24-29
72	☐ 2:1-7	☐ 2:8-15	☐ 2:16-23	☐ 3:1-4	☐ 3:5-15	☐ 3:16-25	☐ 4:1-18
73	☐ I Thes 1:1-3	☐ 1:4-10	☐ 2:1-12	☐ 2:13—3:5	☐ 3:6-13	☐ 4:1-10	☐ 4:11—5:11
74	☐ 5:12-28	☐ II Thes 1:1-12	☐ 2:1-17	☐ 3:1-18	☐ I Tim 1:1-2	☐ 1:3-4	☐ 1:5-14
75	☐ 1:15-20	☐ 2:1-7	☐ 2:8-15	☐ 3:1-13	☐ 3:14—4:5	☐ 4:6-16	☐ 5:1-25
76	☐ 6:1-10	☐ 6:11-21	☐ II Tim 1:1-10	☐ 1:11-18	☐ 2:1-15	☐ 2:16-26	☐ 3:1-13
77	☐ 3:14—4:8	☐ 4:9-22	☐ Titus 1:1-4	☐ 1:5-16	☐ 2:1-15	☐ 3:1-8	☐ 3:9-15
78	☐ Philem 1:1-11	☐ 1:12-25	☐ Heb 1:1-2	☐ 1:3-5	☐ 1:6-14	☐ 2:1-9	☐ 2:10-18

Reading Schedule for the Recovery Version of the New Testament with Footnotes

Wk.	Lord's Day	Monday	Tuesday	Wednesday	Thursday	Friday	Saturday
79	Heb 3:1-6	3:7-19	4:1-9	4:10-13	4:14-16	5:1-10	5:11—6:3
80	6:4-8	6:9-20	7:1-10	7:11-28	8:1-6	8:7-13	9:1-4
81	9:5-14	9:15-28	10:1-18	10:19-28	10:29-39	11:1-6	11:7-19
82	11:20-31	11:32-40	12:1-2	12:3-13	12:14-17	12:18-26	12:27-29
83	13:1-7	13:8-12	13:13-15	13:16-25	James 1:1-8	1:9-18	1:19-27
84	2:1-13	2:14-26	3:1-18	4:1-10	4:11-17	5:1-12	5:13-20
85	I Pet 1:1-2	1:3-4	1:5	1:6-9	1:10-12	1:13-17	1:18-25
86	2:1-3	2:4-8	2:9-17	2:18-25	3:1-13	3:14-22	4:1-6
87	4:7-16	4:17-19	5:1-4	5:5-9	5:10-14	II Pet 1:1-2	1:3-4
88	1:5-8	1:9-11	1:12-18	1:19-21	2:1-3	2:4-11	2:12-22
89	3:1-6	3:7-9	3:10-12	3:13-15	3:16	3:17-18	I John 1:1-2
90	1:3-4	1:5	1:6	1:7	1:8-10	2:1-2	2:3-11
91	2:12-14	2:15-19	2:20-23	2:24-27	2:28-29	3:1-5	3:6-10
92	3:11-18	3:19-24	4:1-6	4:7-11	4:12-15	4:16—5:3	5:4-13
93	5:14-17	5:18-21	II John 1:1-3	1:4-9	1:10-13	III John 1:1-6	1:7-14
94	Jude 1:1-4	1:5-10	1:11-19	1:20-25	Rev 1:1-3	1:4-6	1:7-11
95	1:12-13	1:14-16	1:17-20	2:1-6	2:7	2:8-9	2:10-11
96	2:12-14	2:15-17	2:18-23	2:24-29	3:1-3	3:4-6	3:7-9
97	3:10-13	3:14-18	3:19-22	4:1-5	4:6-7	4:8-11	5:1-6
98	5:7-14	6:1-8	6:9-17	7:1-8	7:9-17	8:1-6	8:7-12
99	8:13—9:11	9:12-21	10:1-4	10:5-11	11:1-4	11:5-14	11:15-19
100	12:1-4	12:5-9	12:10-18	13:1-10	13:11-18	14:1-5	14:6-12
101	14:13-20	15:1-8	16:1-12	16:13-21	17:1-6	17:7-18	18:1-8
102	18:9—19:4	19:5-10	19:11-16	19:17-21	20:1-6	20:7-10	20:11-15
103	21:1	21:2	21:3-8	21:9-13	21:14-18	21:19-21	21:22-27
104	22:1	22:2	22:3-11	22:12-15	22:16-17	22:18-21	

Week 1 — Day 1

Today's verses

Acts 22:15 For you will be a witness to Him unto all men of the things which you have seen and heard.

Acts 26:16 ...I have appeared to you for this *purpose*, to appoint you as a minister and a witness both of the things in which you have seen Me and of the things in which I will appear to you.

Acts 26:19 Therefore, King Agrippa, I was not disobedient to the heavenly vision.

Eph. 3:4-5 By which, in reading *it*, you can perceive my understanding in the mystery of Christ, which in other generations was not made known to the sons of men, as it has now been revealed to His holy apostles and prophets in spirit.

Date

Week 1 — Day 2

Today's verses

Col. 1:25-27 Of which I became a minister according to the stewardship of God, which was given to me for you, to complete the word of God, the mystery which has been hidden from the ages and from the generations but now has been manifested to His saints; to whom God willed to make known what are the riches of the glory of this mystery among the Gentiles, which is Christ in you, the hope of glory.

Date

Week 1 — Day 3

Today's verses

Eph. 3:3-5 That by revelation the mystery was made known to me,...you can perceive my understanding in the mystery of Christ, which in other generations was not made known to the sons of men, as it has now been revealed to His holy apostles and prophets in spirit.

Eph. 3:8-11 To me...was this grace given to announce to the Gentiles the unsearchable riches of Christ as the gospel and to enlighten all *that they may see* what the economy of the mystery is,...in order that now to the rulers and the authorities in the heavenlies the multifarious wisdom of God might be made known through the church, according to the eternal purpose which He made in Christ Jesus our Lord.

Date

Week 1 — Day 4

Today's verses

Rom. 9:23 In order that He might make known the riches of His glory upon vessels of mercy, which He had before prepared unto glory.

2 Cor. 4:7 But we have this treasure in earthen vessels that the excellency of the power may be of God and not out of us.

Eph. 3:19 ...That you may be filled unto all the fullness of God.

Date

Week 1 — Day 5

Today's verses

Col. 2:2 That their hearts may be comforted, they being knit together in love and unto all the riches of the full assurance of understanding, unto the full knowledge of the mystery of God, Christ.

Eph. 3:4 By which, in reading *it*, you can perceive my understanding in the mystery of Christ.

Eph. 3:6 That in Christ Jesus the Gentiles are fellow heirs and fellow members of the Body and fellow partakers of the promise through the gospel.

Eph. 5:32 This mystery is great, but I speak with regard to Christ and the church.

Date

Week 1 — Day 6

Today's verses

Prov. 29:18 Where there is no vision, the people cast off restraint...

Eph. 4:16 Out from whom all the Body, being joined together and being knit together *through* every joint of the rich supply and through the operation in the measure of each one part, causes the growth of the Body unto the building up of itself in love.

Date

Week 2 — Day 4

Today's verses

2 Cor. 3:18   But we all with unveiled face, beholding and reflecting like a mirror the glory of the Lord, are being transformed into the same image from glory to glory, even as from the Lord Spirit.

Rom. 8:4   That the righteous requirement of the law might be fulfilled in us, who do not walk according to the flesh but according to the spirit.

Date

Week 2 — Day 5

Today's verses

Exo. 26:26-28   And you shall make bars of acacia wood, five for the boards of the one side of the tabernacle, and five bars for the boards of the other side of the tabernacle, and five bars for the boards of the side of the tabernacle at the rear westward. And the middle bar shall pass through in the center of the boards from end to end.

Rom. 8:16   The Spirit Himself witnesses with our spirit that we are children of God.

Date

Week 2 — Day 6

Today's verses

Eph. 4:2-3   With all lowliness and meekness, with long-suffering, bearing one another in love, being diligent to keep the oneness of the Spirit in the uniting bond of peace.

Matt. 16:24   Then Jesus said to His disciples, If anyone wants to come after Me, let him deny himself and take up his cross and follow Me.

Date

Week 2 — Day 1

Today's verses

John 17:11   ...Holy Father, keep them in Your name, which You have given to Me, that they may be one even as We are.

Exo. 26:15   And you shall make the boards for the tabernacle of acacia wood, standing up.

29   And you shall overlay the boards with gold, and make their rings of gold as holders for the bars; and you shall overlay the bars with gold.

Eph. 1:13   ...In Him also believing, you were sealed with the Holy Spirit of the promise.

Date

Week 2 — Day 2

Today's verses

John 17:21-23   That they all may be one; even as You, Father, are in Me and I in You, that they also may be in Us; that the world may believe that You have sent Me. And the glory which You have given Me I have given to them, that they may be one, even as We are one; I in them, and You in Me, that they may be perfected into one...

Date

Week 2 — Day 3

Today's verses

Col. 2:19   ...The Head, out from whom all the Body...grows with the growth of God.

Phil. 3:8-10   ...Christ Jesus my Lord, on account of whom I have suffered the loss of all things and count *them* as refuse that I may gain Christ and be found in Him...to know Him and the power of His resurrection and the fellowship of His sufferings, being conformed to His death.

Date

Week 3 — Day 1
Today's verses

Eph. 4:3-4   Being diligent to keep the oneness of the Spirit in the uniting bond of peace: One Body and one Spirit...

John 17:22-23   And the glory which You have given Me I have given to them, that they may be one, even as We are one; I in them, and You in Me, that they may be perfected into one...

Acts 4:24   And when they heard *this*, they lifted up *their* voice with one accord to God...

Date

Week 3 — Day 2
Today's verses

Acts 1:14   These all continued steadfastly with one accord in prayer...

1 Cor. 12:13   For also in one Spirit we were all baptized into one Body, whether Jews or Greeks, whether slaves or free, and were all given to drink one Spirit.

20   But now the members are many, but the body one.

27   Now you are the Body of Christ, and members individually.

Date

Week 3 — Day 3
Today's verses

Acts 1:14   These all continued steadfastly with one accord in prayer...

15:25   It seemed good to us, having become of one accord, to choose men to send to you together with our beloved Barnabas and Paul.

Matt. 18:19   Again, truly I say to you that if two of you are in harmony on earth concerning any matter for which they ask, it will be done for them from My Father who is in the heavens.

Date

Week 3 — Day 4
Today's verses

Prov. 29:18   Where there is no vision, the people cast off restraint...

Acts 26:19   Therefore, King Agrippa, I was not disobedient to the heavenly vision.

Phil. 3:15   Let us therefore, as many as are full-grown, have this mind; and if in anything you are otherwise minded, this also God will reveal to you.

Acts 2:42   And they continued steadfastly in the teaching and the fellowship of the apostles, in the breaking of bread and the prayers.

46   And day by day, continuing steadfastly with one accord in the temple and breaking bread from house to house...

Date

Week 3 — Day 5
Today's verses

Phil. 1:27   ...That you stand firm in one spirit, with one soul striving together *along* with the faith of the gospel.

1 Cor. 1:10   ...That you all speak the same thing and *that* you be attuned in the same mind and in the same opinion.

Rom. 15:5-6   Now the God of endurance and encouragement grant you to be of the same mind toward one another according to Christ Jesus, that with one accord you may with one mouth glorify the God and Father of our Lord Jesus Christ.

Date

Week 3 — Day 6
today's verses

Jer. 32:39   And I will give them one heart and one way, to fear Me all the days, for their own good and for *the good of* their children after them.

Deut. 25:13-15   You shall not have in your bag differing weights, one, heavy and one light. You shall not have in your house differing measures, one large and one small. A full and righteous weight you shall have, *and* a full and righteous measure you shall have, in order that your days may be extended upon the land which Jehovah your God is giving you.

Date

Week 4 — Day 6 — Today's verses

2 Cor. 13:14 The grace of the Lord Jesus Christ and the love of God and the fellowship of the Holy Spirit be with you all.

1 John 1:3 That which we have seen and heard we report also to you that you also may have fellowship with us, and indeed our fellowship is with the Father and with His Son Jesus Christ.

7 But if we walk in the light as He is in the light, we have fellowship with one another, and the blood of Jesus His Son cleanses us from every sin.

Week 4 — Day 3 — Today's verses

Eph. 4:3-4 Being diligent to keep the oneness of the Spirit in the uniting bond of peace: One Body and one Spirit, even as you were called in one hope of your calling.

1 Cor. 12:12-13 For even as the body is one and has many members, yet all the members of the body, being many, are one body, so also is the Christ. For also in one Spirit we were all baptized into one Body...and were all given to drink one Spirit.

Week 4 — Day 5 — Today's verses

Acts 2:42 And they continued steadfastly in the teaching and the fellowship of the apostles, in the breaking of bread and the prayers.

1 Cor. 4:17 Because of this I have sent Timothy to you, who is my beloved and faithful child in the Lord, who will remind you of my ways which are in Christ, even as I teach everywhere in every church.

Week 4 — Day 2 — Today's verses

1 John 1:6-7 If we say that we have fellowship with Him and yet walk in the darkness, we lie and are not practicing the truth; but if we walk in the light as He is in the light, we have fellowship with one another, and the blood of Jesus His Son cleanses us from every sin.

Phil. 2:1 If there is therefore...any fellowship of spirit...

Week 4 — Day 4 — Today's verses

1 Cor. 1:9 God is faithful, through whom you were called into the fellowship of His Son, Jesus Christ our Lord.

10:16-17 The cup of blessing which we bless, is it not the fellowship of the blood of Christ? The bread which we break, is it not the fellowship of the body of Christ? Seeing that there is one bread, we who are many are one Body; for we all partake of the one bread.

Week 4 — Day 1 — Today's verses

Acts 2:42 And they continued steadfastly in the teaching and the fellowship of the apostles...

1 John 1:2-3 (And the life was manifested, and we have seen and testify and report to you the eternal life, which was with the Father and was manifested to us); that which we have seen and heard we report also to you that you also may have fellowship with us, and indeed our fellowship is with the Father and with His Son Jesus Christ.

Week 5 — Day 1

Today's verses

John 4:14 But whoever drinks of the water that I will give him shall by no means thirst forever; but the water that I will give him will become in him a fountain of water springing up into eternal life.

7:38-39 He who believes into Me, as the Scripture said, out of his innermost being shall flow rivers of living water. But this He said concerning the Spirit...

Acts 2:33 Therefore having been exalted to the right hand of God and having received the promise of the Holy Spirit from the Father, He has poured out this which you both see and hear.

Date

Week 5 — Day 2

Today's verses

Psa. 36:9 For with You is the fountain of life; in Your light we see light.

46:4 There is a river whose streams gladden the city of God...

Rev. 22:1 And he showed me a river of water of life, bright as crystal, proceeding out of the throne of God and of the Lamb...

1 Cor. 16:10 Now if Timothy comes, see that he is with you without fear; for he is working the work of the Lord, even as I am.

Date

Week 5 — Day 3

Today's verses

Acts 2:42 And they continued steadfastly in the teaching and the fellowship of the apostles...

1 John 1:3 That which we have seen and heard we report also to you that you also may have fellowship with us, and indeed our fellowship is with the Father and with His Son Jesus Christ.

1 Cor. 10:16 The cup of blessing which we bless, is it not the fellowship of the blood of Christ? The bread which we break, is it not the fellowship of the body of Christ?

2 Cor. 13:14 The grace of the Lord Jesus Christ and the love of God and the fellowship of the Holy Spirit be with you all.

Date

Week 5 — Day 4

Today's verses

1 Cor. 12:24 ...But God has blended the body together, giving more abundant honor to the *member* that lacked.

Rom. 15:7 Therefore receive one another, as Christ also received you to the glory of God.

16:3-4 Greet Prisca and Aquila, my fellow workers in Christ Jesus, who risked their own necks for my life, to whom not only I give thanks, but also all the churches of the Gentiles.

20 Now the God of peace will crush Satan under your feet shortly. The grace of our Lord Jesus be with you.

Date

Week 5 — Day 5

Today's verses

Eph. 4:3-4 Being diligent to keep the oneness of the Spirit in the uniting bond of peace: One Body and one Spirit...

Acts 1:14 These all continued steadfastly with one accord in prayer...

Phil. 1:27 Only, conduct yourselves in a manner worthy of the gospel of Christ...that you stand firm in one spirit, with one soul striving together *along* with the faith of the gospel.

Date

Week 5 — Day 6

Today's verses

Eph. 1:22-23 And He subjected all things under His feet and gave Him *to be* Head over all things to the church, which is His Body...

4:4-6 One Body and one Spirit, even as also you were called in one hope of your calling; one Lord, one faith, one baptism; one God and Father of all, who is over all and through all and in all.

Week 6 — Day 4   Today's verses

John 1:14   And the Word became flesh....

1 Cor. 15:45   ...The last Adam *became* a life-giving Spirit.

Rev. 1:4   ...Grace to you and peace from Him who is and who was and who is coming, and from the seven Spirits who are before His throne.

Date

Week 6 — Day 5   Today's verses

Rev. 3:1   And to the messenger of the church in Sardis write: These things says He who has the seven Spirits of God...

4:5   ...And *there were* seven lamps of fire burning before the throne, which are the seven Spirits of God.

21:2   And I saw the holy city, New Jerusalem, coming down out of heaven from God, prepared as a bride adorned for her husband.

Date

Week 6 — Day 6   Today's verses

Rev. 5:6   And I saw...a Lamb standing as having *just* been slain, having seven horns and seven eyes, which are the seven Spirits of God sent forth into all the earth.

1 Cor. 3:6, 9   I planted, Apollos watered, but God caused the growth....For we are God's fellow workers; you are God's cultivated land, God's building.

16:10   Now if Timothy comes, see that he is with you without fear; for he is working the work of the Lord, even as I am.

Date

Week 6 — Day 1   Today's verses

Eph. 3:9   And to enlighten all *that they may see* what the economy of the mystery is, which throughout the ages has been hidden in God, who created all things.

16-17   That He would grant you, according to the riches of His glory, to be strengthened with power through His Spirit into the inner man, that Christ may make His home in your hearts through faith...

2 Cor. 4:16   Therefore we do not lose heart; but though our outer man is decaying, yet our inner *man* is being renewed day by day.

Date

Week 6 — Day 2   Today's verses

Gal. 1:15-16   But when it pleased God, who set me apart from my mother's womb and called me through His grace, to reveal His Son in me...

2:20   I am crucified with Christ; and *it is* no longer I *who* live, but *it is* Christ *who* lives in me; and the *life* which I now live in the flesh I live in faith...

4:19   My children, with whom I travail again in birth until Christ is formed in you.

1 Cor. 15:58   Therefore, my beloved brothers, be steadfast, immovable, always abounding in the work of the Lord, knowing that your labor is not in vain in the Lord.

Date

Week 6 — Day 3   Today's verses

Eph. 1:22-23   And He...gave Him to be Head over all things to the church, which is His Body...

4:11-12   And He Himself gave some as apostles and some as prophets and some as evangelists and some as shepherds and teachers, for the perfecting of the saints unto the work of the ministry, unto the building up of the Body of Christ.

Date

Week 7 — Day 1

Today's verses

Matt. 16:18 ...I will build My church, and the gates of Hades shall not prevail against it.

John 14:20 In that day you will know that I am in My Father, and you in Me, and I in you....

15:4 Abide in Me and I in you....

Date _____

Week 7 — Day 2

Today's verses

Gen. 1:26 And God said, Let Us make man in Our image, according to Our likeness; and let them have dominion....

1 Tim. 3:15-16 But if I delay, I *write* that you may know how one ought to conduct himself in the house of God, which is the church of the living God, the pillar and base of the truth. And confessedly, great is the mystery of godliness: He who was manifested in the flesh,...

Rev. 21:2 And I saw the holy city, New Jerusalem, coming down out of heaven from God, prepared as a bride adorned for her husband.

Date _____

Week 7 — Day 3

Today's verses

John 3:29-30 He who has the bride is the bridegroom....He must increase...

Col. 2:19 And not holding the Head, out from whom all the Body, being richly supplied and knit together by means of the joints and sinews, grows with the growth of God.

Eph. 3:17, 19 That Christ may make His home in your hearts... that you may be filled unto all the fullness of God.

Date _____

Week 7 — Day 4

Today's verses

John 17:21-23 That they all may be one; even as You, Father, are in Me and I in You, that they also may be in Us; that the world may believe that You have sent Me. And the glory which You have given Me I have given to them, that they may be one, even as We are one; I in them, and You in Me, that they may be perfected into one...

Date _____

Week 7 — Day 5

Today's verses

Ezek. 44:4 Then He brought me through the north gate to the front of the house; and I looked, and just then the glory of Jehovah filled the house of Jehovah, and I fell upon my face.

43:5 And the Spirit took me up and brought me into the inner court; and just then the glory of Jehovah filled the house.

7 And He said to me, Son of man, *this is* the place of My throne and the place of the soles of My feet, where I will dwell in the midst of the children of Israel forever....

Date _____

Week 7 — Day 6

Today's verses

Ezek. 43:10-11 You, O son of man, describe the house to the house of Israel, that they may feel humiliated because of their iniquities, and let them measure the pattern....Make known to them the design of the house, the arrangement, its exits, its entrances, its whole design, and all its statutes—indeed its whole design and all its laws; and write *them* down in their sight, that they may keep its whole design and all its statutes, and do them.

1 Tim. 3:15 But if I delay, I write that you may know how one ought to conduct himself in the house of God, which is the church of the living God...

Date _____

Week 8 — Day 4 — Today's verses

Exo. And God also said to Moses, Thus you
3:15 shall say to the children of Israel, Jehovah, the God of your fathers, the God of Abraham, the God of Isaac, and the God of Jacob, has sent me to you. This is My name forever, and this is My memorial from generation to generation.

Gen. And he believed Jehovah, and He ac-
15:6 counted it to him as righteousness.

25:5 And Abraham gave all that he had to Isaac.

49:28 All these are the twelve tribes of Israel, and this is what their father spoke to them when he blessed them; he blessed them, each one according to his blessing.

Date

Week 8 — Day 5 — Today's verses

Gal. But I say, Walk by the Spirit and you shall
5:16 by no means fulfill the lust of the flesh.
25 If we live by the Spirit, let us also walk by the Spirit.

Col. And have put on the new man, which is
3:10-11 being renewed unto full knowledge according to the image of Him who created him, where...Christ is all and in all.

Date

Week 8 — Day 6 — Today's verses

Gal. For neither is circumcision anything nor
6:15-16 uncircumcision, but a new creation _is what matters_. And as many as walk by this rule, peace be upon them and mercy, even upon the Israel of God.

Rev. And I saw the holy city, New Jerusalem,
21:2 coming down out of heaven from God, prepared as a bride adorned for her husband.

Date

Week 8 — Day 1 — Today's verses

Gal. And as many as walk by this rule, peace
6:16 be upon them and mercy, even upon the Israel of God.

3:26 For you are all sons of God through faith in Christ Jesus.

5:22-23 But the fruit of the Spirit is love, joy, peace, long-suffering, kindness, goodness, faithfulness, meekness, self-control; against such things there is no law.

2 Tim. If we endure, we will also reign with
2:12 Him...

Date

Week 8 — Day 2 — Today's verses

Rom. ...Those who receive the abundance of
5:17 grace and of the gift of righteousness will reign in life through the One, Jesus Christ.

21 In order that just as sin reigned in death, so also grace might reign through righteousness unto eternal life through Jesus Christ our Lord.

Matt. You then pray in this way: Our Father who
6:9-10 is in the heavens, Your name be sanctified; Your kingdom come; Your will be done, as in heaven, _so_ also on earth.

Date

Week 8 — Day 3 — Today's verses

Gen. And God blessed them; and God said to
1:28 them, Be fruitful and multiply, and fill the earth and subdue it, and have dominion...

2:15 And Jehovah God took the man and put him in the garden of Eden to work it and to keep it.

Luke Behold, I have given you the authority to
10:19 tread upon serpents and scorpions and over all the power of the enemy, and nothing shall by any means hurt you.

Rev. And they overcame him because of the
12:11 blood of the Lamb and because of the word of their testimony, and they loved not their soul-life even unto death.

Date

Week 9 — Day 4

Today's verses

1 Cor. 3:9 For we are God's fellow workers; you are God's cultivated land, God's building.

Rev. 21:2 And I saw the holy city, New Jerusalem, coming down out of heaven from God, prepared as a bride adorned for her husband.

19 The foundations of the wall of the city were adorned with every precious stone...

Date

Week 9 — Day 5

Today's verses

2 Cor. 3:18 But we all with unveiled face, beholding and reflecting like a mirror the glory of the Lord, are being transformed into the same image from glory to glory, even as from the Lord Spirit.

S. S. 1:10-11 Your cheeks are lovely with plaits of ornaments, your neck with strings of jewels. We will make you plaits of gold with studs of silver.

Date

Week 9 — Day 6

Today's verses

1 Cor. 3:12-15 But if anyone builds upon the foundation gold, silver, precious stones, wood, grass, stubble, the work of each will become manifest; for the day will declare it, because it is revealed by fire, and the fire itself will prove each one's work, of what sort it is. If anyone's work which he has built upon the foundation remains, he will receive a reward; if anyone's work is consumed, he will suffer loss, but he himself will be saved, yet so as through fire.

Date

Week 9 — Day 1

Today's verses

Rev. 21:10 And he carried me away in spirit onto a great and high mountain and showed me the holy city, Jerusalem, coming down out of heaven from God.

John 4:14 ...The water that I will give him will become in him a fountain of water springing up into eternal life.

Date

Week 9 — Day 2

Today's verses

Rev. 2:7 ...To him who overcomes, to him I will give to eat of the tree of life, which is in the Paradise of God.

3:12 He who overcomes, him I will make a pillar in the temple of My God, and he shall by no means go out anymore, and I will write upon him the name of My God and the name of the city of My God, the New Jerusalem, which descends out of heaven from My God, and My new name.

Date

Week 9 — Day 3

Today's verses

Rev. 21:18 And the building work of its wall was jasper; and the city was pure gold, like clear glass.

21 And the twelve gates were twelve pearls; each one of the gates was, respectively, of one pearl....

22:1-2 And he showed me a river of water of life, bright as crystal, proceeding out of the throne of God and of the Lamb in the middle of its street. And on this side and on that side of the river was the tree of life, producing twelve fruits, yielding its fruit each month...

Date